GRANT WRITING
AS STORYTELLING

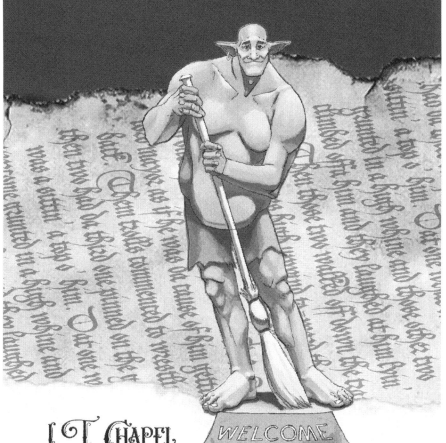

J. T. CHAPEL

Grant Writing as Storytelling

By JT Chapel

Illustrations by Neil Durstweiler

Illustrations of Ox and Wisty by JT Chapel

ISBN: 978-1-7373100-0-6

The Author

JT Chapel wrote grants for 25 plus years earning his clients millions of dollars and maintaining a percentage of over 80% of grants submitted winning awards.

JT was born in Toronto and grew up in California where he attended University and learned how to write grants. Today JT lives in Northern California where he works, hones his writing craft and enjoys morning walks with Ray and George.

Dedicated to Sal who taught me how to write grants and was jealous of his craft. Sal is probably looking down and cursing at me for writing this book because he always told me, "We don't teach people our secrets."

Figure 1 - Angus at Football Practice

Grant Writing as Story Telling

Contents

Preface i

Introduction v

    Elements of a Good Story v

    Parallels in Story Structure vi

    Differences in Composition viii

Abstract><Summary 1

    Village of Abbingdon Troll Abatement Grant Proposal 3

    Village of Abbingdon Troll Abatement Proposal 5

Statement of Need><The Problem 7

    Establishing the Problem 9

    Village of Abbingdon Troll Abatement Proposal 14

Quality of Key Personnel & Adequacy of Resources><The Hero ... 15

    Staff Qualifications 17

    Facilities and Equipment 18

    Location of Services and Personnel 19

    Village of Abbingdon Troll Abatement Proposal 20

    Goals and Objectives><The Quest 20

    Village of Abbingdon Troll Abatement Proposal 25

Program Design><The Solution 27

Description of Activities><Principal Actions 28

Research Base 32

Magic (Innovations) 33

Previous History of Success 36

Village of Abbingdon Troll Abatement Proposal 37

Management Plan/Timeline><Subplot 39

Formats and Content 40

Village of Abbingdon Troll Abatement Grant Proposal 42

Sustainability Plan 43

Village of Abbingdon Troll Abatement Proposal 46

Partnerships and Collaborations 47

Village of Abbingdon Troll Abatement Proposal 48

Evaluation Plan><Beneficiaries 49

Outcome Evaluation 50

Process Evaluation 51

What is the Higher State? 51

Village of Abbingdon Troll Abatement Proposal 52

Budget, Funding &Sustainability><Magic Talisman 53

Village of Abbingdon Troll Abatement Proposal 56

Budget Narrative 57

Appendices 59

Appendix A - Application Guidelines and Instructions 59

Appendix B – Troll Abatement Grant Scoring Rubric 67

Appendix C – Village of Abbingdon Troll Abatement Proposal...75

Appendix D – Abbingdon Grant Evaluation Report 107

Appendix E – Beat Sheet Concept 149

Preface

Grant writing is often taught as a solely technical genre. It is, without a doubt, a *form* of technical writing. Grants follow prescribed formats with technical guidelines restricting their composition; however, grant writing that is purely technical will likely put your audience of readers to sleep. While writing a technically-correct grant is critical, this book is written to focus grant writers and aspiring grant writers on another equally important aspect of grant writing, that of storytelling.

Good grants tell a story, a story about how the applicant will solve a problem. Solving a problem is what stories are about. *The Wizard of Oz* is about how Dorothy found her way back home, and *A Christmas Carol* is a story about how Ebenezer Scrooge found his way back to love. A grant is structured like a fictional story in that it presents the problem to be solved right at the beginning. Dorothy's need to find her way home is presented in the form of a tornado that flies her from Kansas to Oz. The ghost of Marley haunts Scrooge to tell him he has a problem. Similarly, a grant commonly presents the needs to be addressed—the problem—to be solved first. And as with most stories, the rest of a grant narrative is a description of how the protagonist, the applicant, the hero of the story, will use the funds requested to solve the problem or problems, much as Dorothy and Scrooge go through a process, gain knowledge, and leverage resources to solve their problems—Dorothy uses the ruby slippers and Scrooge, somewhat against his will, uses the teachings of the three ghosts.

The chapters in this book describe the most common grant sections found in grant outlines. It also provides an explanation about how to write these sections as well as a grant narrative example. To stress the storytelling theme of the book, the grant narrative example is in the form of a fictional grant application written to request a grant to resolve a frightening problem in a mythical world. The problem is the appearance of dangerous trolls in the Village of Abbingdon on the Isle of Thatch. The entire grant narrative is also included as an appendix.

Additional appendices are included. Examples of the types of documents you may find provided by a grant maker, including the guidelines and instructions (sometimes called a request for proposals), a scoring rubric, and an evaluation report. The evaluation report gives details about how the grant was implemented to provide the reader with a complete picture of how the people of Abbingdon dealt with their troll complications.

The evaluation report is not part of a grant proposal, so the reader may question why it is included here. I can provide two reasons. One is that grants are written to solve a problem through measurable outcomes so it is important for grant writers to understand that real things will be accomplished as a result of their writing. This perspective should influence the grant writer's proposal writing by moderating unreasonable assumptions. An important part of being a successful grant writer is to help guide clients toward realistic planning and designing achievable outcomes. The second reason the evaluation report is included is that after the grant was written, it seemed unfair to the reader to leave the story half-told. It is a fictitious grant, after all, so a fictitious telling of how it worked out made sense. More selfishly, it was fun to write.

The illustrations in this book came about by chance. The author came to know the illustrator Neil as a barista in a coffee shop in Sacramento, California that has long since closed up. He took notice of Neil drawing on his breaks and his talent was obvious. The author inquired if Neil was interested in creating drawings for the book, for a fee and he graciously accommodated the meager project budget and came up with some terrific illustrations.

By way of confession, I've taken liberties with the names of places I've visited in Great Britain throughout the grant narrative. The likely result is that I'll be sentenced to the Tower of London upon my next visit. But the jumbling geography is intentional and I rely on the endless font of good humor among the inhabitants of my ancestral lands.

If this book helps improve your ability to tell a story as part of grant writing, it has achieved its end.

Good storytelling to one and all!

Introduction

Figure 2 – Homeless Cotswalds Troll

Elements of a Good Story

The assertion that grant writing is a form of storytelling may come as a surprise. Often grant writers are trained in grant seminars to think of a grant proposal as nothing more than a descriptive, persuasive technical narrative—more like a how-to manual than *A Tale of Two Cities*. But a grant proposal is truly a genre of story and in this book we'll explore how grant narratives are organized with a structure that mirrors many traditional story structures.

Parallels in Story Structure

The figure below shows the analogous terms between grant structure and the classic story structures so well-documented by Joseph Campbell, Christopher Vogler, and James Bonnet. This list of terms serves as our book outline and will guide our study. Each following chapter addresses one of these story structures and describes it in terms of grant writing while emphasizing its relationship to the story analog.

Grants >	< Stories
Abstract >	< Summary
Statement of Need >	< The Problem
Who We Are & Adequacy of Resources >	< The Hero
Goals and Objective >	< The Quest
Program Design >	< The Solution
Evaluation Plan >	< Beneficiaries
Management Plan >	< Subplot
Budget & Sustainability >	< Magic Talisman

Abstract><Summary – This section is just what it sounds like: a short, concise overview, an appetizer if you will, that is meant to give the reader a delicious, savory taste of the plot to whet the appetite and make them want more. In a fiction book, think of the fly cover summary of the book as the abstract, it is a short dense narrative written to entice you to read the whole narrative.

Statement of Need><Problem – A story is not a story without a problem to solve, and a grant is not a grant without a need (problem) to resolve.

<u>Who We Are & Adequacy of Resources</u>><u>The Hero</u> — A hero's quest is undertaken by a protagonist, and that hero has to be capable of completing the quest. Reader trust in the hero is especially important when the tasks they'll perform during the quest require character development, resources or magic along the path.

<u>Goals & Objectives</u>><u>The Quest</u> — The next part of a grant story is to define the desired parameters and outcomes of the quest. Unlike a traditional story, a grant narrative is expected to give the reader the anticipated ending right up front. Grants are not a mystery genre, and narratives written as such fail to win funding.

<u>Program Design</u>><u>The Solution</u> — This is the section of a grant in which the writer describes the activities the hero will undertake during the journey to a solution.

<u>Evaluation Plan</u>>< <u>Beneficiaries</u> — This part of the story tells the reader how we'll know who or what benefits are accrued by the grant activities. In this section, the grant writer presents a detailed plan to measure the results of the quest. A detailed plan is written to present the specific means and methods that will be used to assess achievement based on measurements spelled out in the goals and objectives.

<u>Budget & Funding</u>><u>Magic Talisman</u> — A grant award acts as a magic talisman that enables the hero to embark on the quest. In many stories the hero must obtain a talisman to achieve the goal of the quest. In *Star Wars*, "the Force" was the talisman that enabled Luke Skywalker to achieve his quest. Dorothy wore her talisman, the ruby slippers. Grant funds, like a talisman in a story, are an absolute necessity for a successful grant quest.

Incorporating the story structures above into a grant narrative makes it stronger. When a grant writer incorporates knowledge of these story structures, an otherwise bland narrative can be transformed into a powerful story. When this is done, the reader not only interprets the factual information provided but also experiences the story it tells on a level they may not consciously recognize. Classic story structure leverages the reader's unconscious understanding of stories that is innate to human experience.

Differences in Composition

Fiction writers have a great deal of artistic license about how to treat each story element. The grant writer does not have this luxury but instead must work within the restrictions set forth in the guidelines and instructions, also called a request for proposals (RFP) or a request for applications (RFA).

The grant writer must work skillfully within published grant guidelines. The writer's goal is to describe each story element to inform the reader about the hero and the quest. The description provides details about the capacity, location, experience, and capabilities of the applicant agency, and the skill sets and background of the personnel who will lead the quest.

Another challenge for grant writes is that they almost always work within a restricted page limit to tell the story. Within this limit, the writer must present the problem and the expected outcomes of the quest, and convince the reader that the methods to be employed guarantee the hero will triumph.

A grant story must be convincing in real-world terms—and by the end of the grant narrative, the reader must believe the quest is achievable and the hero is capable of undertaking the journey.

When a grant narrative is successful, the reader is motivated to help the hero. They will choose to grant the resources necessary to bring about the higher state of being the applicant's proposal seeks to achieve.

All narratives—whether written to thrill a movie-going audience or to persuade a charitable foundation to open its checkbook—succeed by telling an engaging story to an audience that identifies with the problem and cares about its characters. Grant writers who understand this and use it to elevate their narratives from dry recitations of data to compelling stories have a huge advantage over the competition. And make no mistake, the competition for funding for grants these days is fierce—and becoming more ferocious all the time.

Grant writing success depends more than ever on standing out from the crowd with a proposal that not only crosses all the technical *T*s and dots all the implementation *I*s, but one that also includes a narrative that ignites the reader's imagination with an inspiring story about a hero's journey to triumph over a problem that desperately needs to be solved.

Every working grant writer—and all aspiring grant writers, too—will benefit from understanding the essential nature of story and from learning to apply the storyteller's craft to their grants. To do this, it is vital to know the basic elements of story structure, to understand how a story is developed, and to practice integrating classic story structure into planning a grant narrative.

Did you know that story means narrative?

sto·ry[1]

[stawr-ee, stohr-ee] noun, plural -ries, verb, -ried, -ry·ing. noun

1. A narrative, either true or fictitious, in prose or verse, designed to interest, amuse, or instruct the hearer or reader; tale.

The implication of this definition is important for a grant writer because a narrative that neglects to tell a good story will be lifeless and lifeless grants are often gathering dust on the shredding pile of unfunded proposals. At first glance it may appear that applying this definition to grant writing is overly ambitious, or pretentious, or even off-target, especially when it comes to the notion of "amusing" the reader. But grant writers who have assisted in a grant scoring process know firsthand the difference between an engaging grant story and a dry technical document.

By focusing on the established structure that underlies all good stories, a grant writer can create a proposal that leaps off the page with vitality, inspiring the reader with a hero's journey that resonates because it connects the reader to traditional story structures that humans share and understand.

Grants cannot be written in the highly descriptive and metaphoric language that some readers enjoy in a fictional story. But an engaging narrative can be spare. Think of Ernest Hemingway's compelling stories, such as his oft-anthologized "The Short, Happy Life of Francis Macomber."

---

[1] Definition.com - http://dictionary.reference.com/browse/story, accessed 10/18/11

"Spare" doesn't have to mean "dry!" And while grant writers avoid using overly descriptive sentences, even grant writing is strengthened by what James Bonnet[2] refers to as "conjuring"— finding the right words and concepts to paint vivid pictures in the reader's mind. Grant writers use language artfully, but judiciously, to present the problem, describe the quest, and to propose resolutions in a way that is truthful, yet that emphasizes the elements that make the point in a forceful and persuasive manner.

A dry narrative fails to tap into a reader's emotions and excite their imagination. A narrative that does not speak to universal truths about the human condition, linking these truths to the story's problem and solution, will fail to engage the reader. The design quality of a program may be excellent, but an excellent design only places a grant in competition with the other grants which also present an excellent design. Grants that interest, inform, and—yes—perhaps even amuse the reader are more likely to be awarded funds.

By focusing on the essential story told within a grant proposal, the writer can establish a personal connection with the readers, encouraging them to see the flesh and blood people whose lives can be touched for the better if only they, the readers, and the funding source they represent, say, "Yes—we will join with you in this quest."

The next chapter talks about the first part of a grant, the abstract. So let's jump right into writing that grant story!

---

[2] Bonnet, James. *Stealing Fire from the Gods: The Complete Guide to Story for Writers and Filmmakers* (2nd Edition), 2006. Michael Weise Productions.

Abstract><Summary

Grants often require a one-page abstract that is sometimes part of the scoring, but often not scored. Even if an abstract is not part of the scoring rubric, it is often a required component for a complete application. That it is not scored does not mean the writer should underestimate its value.

I've worked with readers (rather troll-ish ones) who refused to read any narrative or attachments that are not scored. Whether this decision was on a principle of "fairness" or mere laziness I don't know, but if a grant writer put an important fact or feature into the abstract and left it out of the scored narrative, the troll-ish reader's understanding of the quest was impaired and the reader scored the grant lower than they would have if the information was included in the grant narrative instead of only in the abstract. So be careful about this point, don't consider a required or important element "done and dusted" because you included it in an unscored abstract.

An abstract is a concise, tightly written summary of the proposal in which the writer provides the reader with the big picture of the proposal. This can be challenging. Imagine trying to summarize a 50–100 page narrative in one page!

An abstract does more than a fictional story summary because it must describe the problem, the quest, and the expected outcomes. While a story summary scrupulously avoids giving away clues to "the end of the story," the general purpose of both an abstract and a story summary is to entice the reader to keep on reading. A good abstract does this while also giving a reader their first glimpse of the quality of the proposal. Don't hurry through your creation of this part of the proposal, a weak abstract does not instill confidence in the reader.

Figure 3 – Content Cotswalds Troll in Natural Habitat

A simple outline can help you get focused. The proposal narrative's big picture can often be organized using five key elements.

- Establish the problem

Your narrative here should give details like, where the problem is, who is impacted and what that impact is, the scope of the problem, the duration of the problem, and so on. You want to tightly pack this paragraph to make the readers sit up and take interest.

- Identify the applicant

This is a bit of an elevator speech about the hero, who they are, what they do, length of time they've been doing it, who they work with that makes them especially qualified, etc.

- Identify goals and objectives

Depending on how many goals and objectives you're proposing, you may either need to provide a summary or you may be able include all of them. Space will determine how specific you can be.

- Summarize the solutions

Describe briefly how the needs will be met, who-what-when-where is always a good guide.

- Define the measures of success

This is the "how much" of your proposal. Will you increase reading scores by 5 or 10 percentile points on average? Will you create a troll-safe environment in which the children are safe from being stewed? Will you measure success by establishment of an evaluation team?

The last thing to think about when writing the abstract is that these short proposal descriptions are often what the funder uses on their web site as descriptions of funded proposals. The fact that this piece of the grant writer's narrative may become public-facing is another good reason to do some excellent writing on the abstract.

Village of Abbingdon Troll Abatement Grant Proposal

Read the Abstract in Appendix C

Opening

Books often begin with a preface and introduction, or at the very least have an enticing summary on the fly leaf. A grant benefits from a similar introduction so it is wise to insert an opening paragraph in the first page of narrative, regardless of what section that happens to be. I recommend this because as discussed in the previous chapter about abstracts, the abstract is not always a part of what is scored and it helps the reader to understand the proposal context before reading the first section.

Writers should never forget that all narratives are written to be read and interpreted by an audience. Readers have an understanding of story structure from years of listening to oral stories, reading books, literary publications, newspapers and magazines, so a grant writer can tap into that understanding of story structure to give their narrative a natural story flow that even a troll can understand.

The opening paragraph of a grant application is kind of a summary of your abstract; a summary of your summary, if you will. The opening accomplishes some of the same purposes as a fictional introduction: it establishes physical location (setting), it defines the need/problem, and in a grant it also defines the solution and describes the higher state to be achieved by the quest.

An effective story opening immediately draws the reader in; it describes the setting and the main characters. The opening gives the reader context and helps them begin to organize and conceptualize the story in their mind. The main purpose of an opening is to "hook" the reader and make them care about what comes next.

Pushing the reader's "care button" is why grant writers need to include an opening paragraph even if it is not a requirement of an RFP outline. It is almost treasonous to suggest diverting from the outline in the RFP and I can't stress strenuously enough that you are to stick to the prescribed outline in all other aspects. I urge you to divert from the outline in this one tiny exception. *This is the only place I ever deviate from the RFP,* ever, Ever, EVER! ... and if you live by this rule, you too shall live happily ever after.

Because an opening is not usually required—and because each narrative is limited in the number of pages—openings should be restricted to one short, concise paragraph. Because readers unconsciously expect to receive this type of information when they read a story, I have never experienced any negative consequences by including it. An experienced reader will unconsciously think, "Yes, good, now I know what to expect, tell me more."

Village of Abbingdon Troll Abatement Proposal

> *Read the opening paragraph of the*
> *Needs Section in Appendix C*

Statement of Need><The Problem

In the *Wizard of Oz*, Dorothy runs away from home to get away from her troubles, then she is whisked away to Oz by a tornado. Dorothy's problem is established first, she's unhappy at home. As a fictional story often presents the problem at the beginning, the needs section of grants is usually section one. In grant terminology, the analogue for *problem* is *needs*. Just as stories are about solving a problem, grants are given to resolve unmet needs.

Since most grants start with a needs sections, that is where I write an opening paragraph that functions as a concise abstract. I do this even when the abstract is part of the scoring rubric, which it often is not.

The section one position of the needs makes it critical to a successful application. The narrative must be clear and compelling to help the reader understand and empathize with the "state of misfortune." A compelling, factual description of the unfortunate circumstances will help cement the reader's concern, spark their empathy, and clarify the connection of the quest to the funding agency's purpose. Always remember that the grant is provided for the funder's purpose not the grant seeker's purpose; when the two purposes align, the proposal has a chance to receive funding. But if the reader is not compelled to care, understand, and connect with the needs the quest seeks to resolve, you've lost the competition in the first section.

Figure 4 - Dipped but not Stewed in 6th Grade

In order to write a compelling needs section the writer must master the facts of the situation. The truth about the state of misfortune may be supported by facts, data, research, and anecdotal description. The view of the problem may also be enhanced by examples, references to case studies, scans of published quotations, or news articles (but only if it fits within the page restrictions).

In the troll grant, the facts support and validate the state of misfortune. The writer lists statistics on the numbers of trolls that pose a threat, the number of children at risk, the number of children who trolls have attempted to stew over a period of time, and environmental factors such as lack of sufficient troll habitat.

You must provide enough context to help the reader identify with the victims. Admittedly, the troll grant needs are easy, who wouldn't care about children in danger of being stewed by trolls? Your description must include a vivid portrayal of the state of misfortune that steels the reader for the quest. Our goal is to inspire the reader to swear allegiance to the quest because it would be unconscionable not to do so.

If the writer loses the story thread after writing the needs section, the reader will find themselves lost in a narrative that leaves them adrift, confused, and ready to abandon the hero. All of the subsequent grant sections must relate back to addressing and resolving the needs. Too many grant writers lose the plot after they write the needs and they begin writing about solving other needs that were never part of section one. That's a recipe for an unfunded proposal and is usually caused by the actual needs of the applicant being out of alignment with the needs presented.

One last point here, don't assume the reader will make the mental connection between the purposes of the funder in offering the grants to the needs presented in your grant. Explicitly tell the reader how the needs addressed match the purpose of the funding agency. See if you can find on pages 104 where the sample grant provides the reader with that connection.

Establishing the Problem

The threat is portrayed and made real by examples of how not addressing the needs inflicts harm on its victims. For example, a grant writer who writes a grant to teach reading in a neighborhood school may illustrate the need using statistics about the local adult reading levels, unemployment and poverty statistics within the community, and citing research linking these data. If lack of reading ability in adults is linked to negative outcomes, the heightened importance of ensuring that children learn to read becomes apparent to the reader. A subtle but important function of the needs section is to give hope that the value being pursued is not imagined, but attainable and sustainable. Linking the needs to big ideas, like solving unemployment or poverty, are powerful emotive connections and help the reader understand the stakes involved in solving the problem.

quin·tes·sen·tial   [kwin-tuh-sen-shuhl] adjective

1. Representing the perfect example of a class or quality (https://www.vocabulary.com/dictionary/quintessential)

Stories are most interesting when among the possible range of problems, from mild to outrageously bad, a problem is quintessential. How interesting would *King Kong* have been if King Kong was a mildly mischievous spider monkey? A spider monkey is not a quintessential problem in the possible range of primate problems. A story about an average problem, a mediocre threat, a mildly frightening villain, is boring. In the movie *Animal House,* the dean of the university wants to get rid of Delta House as a fraternity on campus so he plots to accomplish this goal with the student president of a rival fraternity. Dean Wormer suggests that Delta House should be put on probation but the student reminds him that the fraternity is already on probation. In keeping with making the story problem quintessential, Dean Wormer declares he'll place Delta on "double-secret probation" thereby creating a quintessential problem for Delta, it's perfect, doubly dangerous *and it's* "double-secret!" That allows the viewer to understand what Delta does not, that their position at the university is much more precarious than they know.

The grant writer must do their utmost to portray needs as quintessential problems. Remember that all applicants present their needs too, so presenting needs in the most urgent terms produces a higher score and a more convincing narrative. Needs are best portrayed as quintessential when the writer does the following things:

1. Maintains focus on the needs to be solved.
2. Uses valid, verifiable data from trusted, reputable sources.
3. Connects the reader to the victims through anecdotal descriptions and specific victim data.
4. Compares the needs to be solved with the needs of similar locations or populations—but only when it is a favorable comparison.
5. Presents needs as they have changed over time—again, only if this is a favorable analysis to presenting the current need.
6. Connects the need to broader issues such as documenting that improvement of a child's reading ability leads to better outcomes as adults.

A quintessential problem is more difficult to solve and a more difficult problem implies more urgency for the reader. This is powerful because quintessential problems engage the reader's imagination more deeply and tap powerful emotions of empathy and hope.

The reader of a grant is tasked with finding the most worthy hero proposing an achievable quest; they must determine upon whom they will bestow the marvelous element of funding. The reader is more likely to bestow it for a great quest than for an average, mundane quest.

In *Jurassic Park*, the quintessential predator was the T-Rex. In *The Wizard of Oz* the quintessential personification of evil was the Wicked Witch of the West who, as the Good Witch Glenda remarked was, "...much worse," than the Wicked Witch of the East who Dorothy's house landed on. Imagine how the story would have been compromised if the quintessential witch had been crushed under the house at the opening of the movie! The threat to Dorothy and her friends would have been far less interesting.

Portraying the needs as quintessential forces the reader to sit up and take notice, to care about the victims, to understand the scope, reach, and threat of the problem and to marvel at the courage of the hero on their quest. In spite of the quintessential evil witch who said, "I'll get you my pretty," Dorothy still began her quest to find her way home following the spiral of the yellow brick road. We were all worried when Dorothy left the safety of Munchkinland and we all knew that the Wicked Witch was waiting for her down that yellow brick road.

Finally, there are a few tips to remember for presenting the needs. Education research tells us that not everyone learns the same way. Some people are visual learners who learn best by seeing pictures, graphs, charts, etc. Some people with different learning styles, like kinesthetic learners; those who learn best by working with their hands, can't always be accommodated in writing but if you're sending in physical copies of your grant, print it on high-quality paper that feels good in your hand. So think about how to best accommodate all learning styles in ways that are amenable to a print document. Sometimes the best way to describe a need is visually, with a graph comparing a need over time or comparing the need related to demographics. Tables and graphs are useful tools to visually punch up an important piece of data. Tables and graphs also break up the text which, if you're reading a pile of grants for a competition, is welcome eye-relief!

A couple of tips on tables and graphs.

- Tables don't always have to conform to the formatting requirements because funders know that a double-spaced table is just a silly waste of space. This can enable you to add a lot of information in a more compressed space. If the RFP of a grant narrative dictates double-spacing, check the RFP carefully to see if this also applies to tables. If there is no explicit language excluding tables, you should reach out to the funder to clarify that question. Lacking something in writing from the funder about spacing in tables, you must assume the spacing would have to conform to the dictates of the RFP. But if you are allowed to use single spacing or reduced-size fonts in tables, do so with caution. Anything you do to make reading the proposal hard for the reader will impact your scores.

- Graphs are nice but consume a lot of space, so use them with discretion. At the end of the writing process when you are trying to squeeze down your narrative to fit within the confined page restriction, you may have to edit out some of these jewels and summarize the data in narrative form.

- Whether you use a table or a graph, you must always, always, always preface it with a short, concise description that points out to the reader *what it tells them* about the needs. It is a mistake to assume the reader will "know" what you intended a visual element to tell them.

A few other tips about the needs section.

- Avoid graphics that have color or that use color to convey specific information. Don't assume that readers will be provided with color copies for scoring. If you use color, make sure it prints out in black and white and is still visually comprehensible.

- Avoid infographics or grant-themed graphics that try to portray the colorful name of the project in a visual format. Often grant writers make up a name for a grant that can be condensed into a nifty acronym. Something like **R**eading **I**mprovement = **S**tudent **E**xcellence; Project R.I.=S.E. for short. That sort of title can be an effective mnemonic to help readers recall your grant during scoring. But trying to turn R.I.=S.E. into a cool graphic is a waste of time and it won't improve your score. Also, graphics are space-eaters and may not be understood, appreciated (beauty is in the eye of the beholder) or taken into account in the scoring. These kinds of graphics are fun to create but end up being a waste of your precious writing time. Always remember that what is written is scored, decoration isn't scored.

Now that you have presented the story problem to the reader in exacting detail and quintessential prose, it is time to tell them who will lead the quest and how the quest will unfold. The next chapter is about how to describe the hero.

Village of Abbingdon Troll Abatement Proposal

Read the Needs Section in Appendix C

Quality of Key Personnel & Adequacy of Resources><The Hero

We've established that grants are about telling stories that solve problems presented vividly and urgently in the needs section. In your grant's story, the applicant is the protagonist, and in a grant, the literary term antagonist is analogous to the needs. All the narrative following the needs section must tell a convincing story that leads the grant reader to believe it is possible for the applicant to defeat the antagonist and resolve the needs, they must be persuaded to believe in the quest.

In this section of the grant the writer introduces the hero. I find this section's location in the grant outline is inconsistent from grant to grant but I placed it here because it is a logical place in terms of storytelling. The narrative outline is prescribed in the application guidelines and instructions or request for proposals (RFP), and these documents, *not this book*, guide organization of your narrative.

Do not forget the grant writer's cardinal rule about following directions!

In describing the protagonist of the story, whether it be the principal investigator or lead researcher, an executive director, possibly even an agency or government office, the writer must describe the characteristics, capacities, and abilities of the hero as these qualities relate to their ability to complete the quest.

Figure 5 - Lord Mayor Gittins

I'll keep reminding you that you're writing for an audience of readers. Consider that these people may or may not know much about the purpose of the grant program, about the solutions you propose, or the applicant. If grant reading assignments are carefully given, the reader won't know anything about the hero. In a national grant competition, the readers are likely to be spread out all over the country and, to avoid potential bias or potential conflicts of interest, the grants are distributed geographically to ensure readers are assigned proposals from states other than their own. Grant readers also agree to recuse themselves from reading grants to which they have any connection, involvement, or familiarity.

Many details can be used to describe the capabilities of an agency to support the argument that the hero is especially well prepared to overcome the challenges and meet the needs. These may include, staff qualifications; facilities and equipment; and location of services. These topics are described below.

Staff Qualifications

Some RFPs include a narrative section titled, "Qualifications of Key Personnel" where you are to write narrative describing the heroes of your story, including staff members who are to fill key positions funded by the grant budget. When a staff member is not pre-identified, the qualifications of the perfect candidate are often summarized instead.

When a person is already identified, you can summarize the qualifications of this individual by describing their educational background, related work experience, awards, publications, etc. If allowed or not specifically prohibited, a principal investigator should provide a curriculum vitae to add as an appendix. But as with all material that isn't scored, be sure to include enough detail in the scored narrative to receive maximum scoring on the assumption that unscored material won't be read (beware of trolls).

A convincing narrative about the hero supports the reader's confidence in your quest. You wouldn't want to give money for a grant to implement troll abatement to a project implemented by a superintendent who knew nothing about trolls. You'd expect the applicant to propose leadership by a seasoned troll expert. After all, the village children's safety is at stake!

The qualifications of the agency must also be touted. Perhaps it has licensure, years of experience and success, consistent leadership, famous board members, in-kind capacities, or awards that can be cited as evidence of sound operations, management, and foremost, the ability to support a successful quest to address the needs and solve the problems.

Facilities and Equipment

If existing facilities and equipment are required for the quest, it's wise to insert narrative description about how those things are to be utilized and committed to the project, this shows readiness of the agency to implement the solutions proposed. Remember also to insert details about those things in the in-kind budget because they represent substantial contributions to the cost of the project and demonstrate commitment.

In the troll abatement grant, children and adults will enroll in troll safety classes, so use of community resources where those classes will be held is described. If we failed to mention these classes would be held in the community hall and the school, it could raise a question in the readers' minds about where these classes would be held and the possibility that lack of facilities and proper planning could cause them not to happen at all.

A strong grant narrative tells a story that answers questions. A professional grant writer anticipates the questions their story will raise in the readers' minds. Experience as a grant reader reinforces your understanding of the reader's thought process and that is a valuable perspective for a grant writer. Seek out and accept invitations to participate in a scoring process for granting agencies and organizations.

Failure to address obvious questions about the implementation of activities such as the provision of meeting space may raise questions in the minds of the readers about the proposal's viability. One of the greatest challenges for a professional grant writer is writing detail-dense narrative and keeping a focus on the *how* of implementation.

If equipment owned by the agency will be utilized for the activities, then point out the quality of manufacture, the sophistication of its technology, its state of repair, the ability of the organization to maintain it, and the degree to which it is considered state-of-the-art within the industry.

Location of Services and Personnel

If the applicant's headquarters is outside the immediate area of need, the hero may need to establish their capacity to provide services in the area of need for the duration of the quest. This may be unnecessary if there are geographic restrictions on applications.

In our troll grant, the stonemasons must set up construction sites on both shores of the Firth of Forth for the entire project year. The stonemasons submitting proposals for the contract will have to show that they have the capability to source and to move materials and equipment to the sites. The Village of Abbingdon would be remiss to omit a statement in their application that they intend to employ stonemasons who can demonstrate full capability to build the bridge. Readers of the grant proposal want to be assured that the writer has considered such details and has described them in the proposal. It is a mistake to project your own positive opinion of the proposal on the grant reader or you'll leave out important details; rather, write for the skeptical perspective, for the reader who won't believe you thought about a detail that isn't included in the narrative.

Now that you have presented a hero that gives your reader confidence, you are ready to tell them about the outcomes your quest will achieve in the goals and objectives section.

Village of Abbingdon Troll Abatement Proposal

*Read the Quality of Key Personnel
section in Appendix C*

So, let's keep in mind the need to present skeptical readers with detail about how the project will unfold into the next chapter, "Program Design," where you will write your quest as a refreshing, motivating narrative description.

Goals and Objectives><The Quest

The parameters of the quest are first defined by the goals and objectives which are often included in a section that is called program design. Goals and objectives are the building blocks on which to plan the quest and form the skeleton of your grant proposal design. The primary story elements addressed in this chapter are the nature of the quest and the higher state to be attained that are expressed by a goal, or goals, and further elucidated in the objectives which I recommend you write in a specific and commonly accepted format.

That goals and objectives often follow the needs section is logical since the problem to be solved was just described. Just as it is important for the needs section to grab the reader by the heart, the goals and objectives appeal to the readers' logical minds. Goals and objectives are critical to establish a proposal framework the readers can agree is logical and leads to a solution of the problem. After experiencing the emotions of your needs section, the reader looks for comfort in outcomes that solve the problem. The primary purpose in the rest of your narrative is to tell a story that puts the reader's fears, questions, and doubts to rest.

Your goals and objectives must answer the reader's next question, which is:

"What are they going to do about these needs to re-solve the state of misfortune?"

The project goal should broadly address the state of misfortune, as in the troll grant example.

Project Goal – Provide the residents of Abbingdon and the Shire of Arbuckle with a troll-safe environment.

Note the broadness of this goal and the lack of specificity. It tells the reader nothing about how achievement of this goal might be measured; measurements are an important component of objectives.

The state of misfortune on the Isle of Thatch is about an unsafe environment. Children are in danger of being stewed by trolls and the unsafe environment threatens the island's thatch industry.

Good objectives are often described by grant writers as being SMART: Specific—Measurable—Achievable—Realistic—Time-Bound.

The following graphic provides more detail about this commonly accepted objective structure.

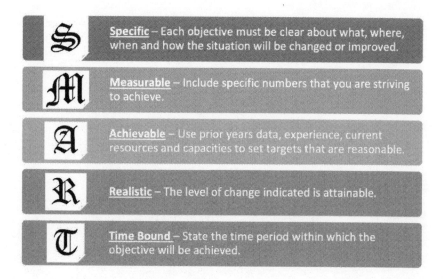

Specific – Each objective must be clear about what, where, when and how the situation will be changed or improved.

Measurable – Include specific numbers that you are striving to achieve.

Achievable – Use prior years data, experience, current resources and capacities to set targets that are reasonable.

Realistic – The level of change indicated is attainable.

Time Bound – State the time period within which the objective will be achieved.

An effective set of objectives provides a framework that leads readers on a logical and measurable pathway toward resolving the state of misfortune. The state of misfortune on the Isle of Thatch cannot be resolved through objectives that are unrelated to producing a troll-safe environment. For example, the following three objectives would cause the reader to lose faith in the quest.

> Objective 1 – By the third month of the project, all residents on the Isle of Thatch will be provided with cable television and flat screen TVs as measured by project surveys, records of equipment distribution, and island ratings of *Doc Martin.*

> Objective 2 – During the 12 months of the project, all trolls will be given injections against troll foot fungus as measured by records of injections given and medical visits related to the fungus.

> Objective 3 – By the end of the project period, a survey shall be taken of the residents of the Isle of

Thatch regarding their preferences for prime minister, their party affiliation, and volunteer hours making sandwiches at a campaign headquarters.

Each of these objectives may address a state of misfortune—poor television reception on the island (which a reader here may interpret as good fortune), rampant foot fungus among the trolls of the island, and the interest of participation in the political process. But not one of them has anything to do with the state of misfortune described in the needs section, and importantly, the objectives do not address the purpose of the funder that issued the RFP. These objectives would disqualify the application as clearly off the mark. When reading grants, you may well find off the mark objectives that address a need that is clearly outside the funder's stated purposes. As a professional grant writer, it is an ethical responsibility not to be coerced to include such objectives and items in the budget. Do not include objectives that do not support a program design that resolves the described needs.

The objectives included in the proposal are designed to support resolution of the state of misfortune. The reader should be thinking:

"Yes, that should work. Now I can see how the state of misfortune can be resolved!"

Your objectives must address the essential methods for addressing the needs. Be certain you don't leave out any important factors central to resolving the state of misfortune. For example, perhaps there is an objective that contributes in an important way to a resolution of a need but some other agency will contribute those resources to support that objective, you must still include that objective. You can clarify later in the program design section—and in the budget narrative—that the funding or resources are provided by other sources.

When including commitments from other sources, the applicant should include a memorandum of understanding (MOU) with that entity that spells out the specific contribution the parties committed to provide. An MOU is an agreement, a form of contract, agreed to by two or more entities and approved and executed by someone with signature authority for an organization, or more often by a governing board. MOUs commit resources toward some purpose, are usually time-limited, and an MOU may be legally enforceable.

A good set of goals and objectives are easily linked to the needs section in the mind of the reader. None of the objectives should raise questions by addressing needs that are not described, or worse, which are not applicable at all to the purpose of the grant or the stated purposes of the funding agency.

If there is space to do so, it is wise to put goals and objectives into a table with a timeline and a column where you can show linkage to the goals of the guidelines and instructions or RFP. At the risk of repetition, remember that you are writing for an audience of readers who don't want to be forced to think *for your application.* Your job is to think for the skeptical reader, to lay out explicit connections between your proposal and the published funding priorities.

I remember from my own reading experiences how tired I was at the end of a particularly difficult week of reading proposals. When I was mentally exhausted from wrestling with bad narratives or trollish readers in the team, the last proposal I read had better be good because my patience for a bad or even a mediocre proposal was stretched very, very thin. If the writer of that last proposal made me think too hard, their score suffered. I was too tired to do their work for them. Write as if your proposal will be the last one read by a tired and cranky grant reader; in this position, yours must be the cold canteen of water saving the life of a reader who just spent a week crawling through a scorching desert of awful, dusty and desiccated proposals.

Village of Abbingdon Troll Abatement Proposal

Read the Goals and Objectives in Appendix C

Program Design><The Solution

The program design (design) is a detailed description of activities that will be undertaken by the hero or deployed by partner organizations to solve the needs and achieve the goal. This section is the roadmap for the quest, the pathway your hero will take to achieve the objectives.

This book does not specifically address the needs of a research grant writer seeking to fund an experimental design, that is, a grant written to test some experimental hypothesis as opposed to implementing a research-based program model. This book addresses that latter grant model, so the design's effectiveness must be validated by citing credible, published evidence of success in similar application of the proposed model by other heroes. This is most often achieved citing specific, current and relevant research-based sources.

The design section gives details about the principal actions of the hero, and magic may be introduced into the narrative as innovations that are new and unique to the hero's quest—more about the hazards of introducing magic later. When innovations are proposed, the magic can distinguish the hero as uniquely qualified to pursue the quest and solve the problem. The research base cited can cement the reader's belief that magic is possible. It is the writer's job to write about this research in a way that links the proposed innovations to the credible research in a way that the reader can make the connection. If you make the reader question whether the research is relevant to the innovation, they may not believe in the magic.

Figure 6 - Inspection of the Troll Watch Volunteers

Description of Activities><Principal Actions

The design must be detailed enough to help the reader understand what will be done, when, and by whom. A design section that causes a reader to ask themselves,

"How will this activity be done?"

is likely to be a losing proposal.

A principal action may be thought of as key activities supporting the objectives. What will be done to achieve the objectives, by whom, for how long, and to what degree? Going back to Dorothy, she would not have written a grant to walk only as far as the Haunted Forest; Dorothy's principal actions were everything she did from the moment she struck out on the Yellow Brick Road from Munchkin Land to find her way home. Your description of principal actions makes the design real in the minds of the readers. A good design section helps the reader see that there is indeed a Yellow Brick Road leading to the completion of your quest.

Many writers lose the opportunity for an award by losing points in the design section even when the needs are quintessential and the goals and objectives are strong. It's a common mistake among novice writers to write about the "WHAT" but not the "HOW" of the design activities. Writing about the "How" is hard, it takes imagination, understanding, and strong communication with the applicant. Writing the "How" is especially hard when grant planning is insufficient. A grant writer must press their clients for answers to how things will get done. If the grant writer does not clarify this with their client, they risk either writing with insufficient detail, or inserting details from their own imagination, and as we've already determined, imaginative freelancing in the grant narrative on behalf of the applicant without their input is dangerous territory for a grant writer, and it is not ethical.

Here's an example of two ways to write about an activity description from the troll abatement grant, the first is a weak narrative for adult troll safety education and the second one is a stronger example from the proposal.

The first description of the adult troll safety education program gives only the what, and the second description from the proposal gives the what and how.

Adult Troll Safety Education – Weak Narrative

All adults will take troll safety education classes and earn their troll safety certificates. Classes will be held at the village community building and a curriculum will be purchased using grant funding. Childcare will be provided for the adults with children.

This narrative tells what is planned, but it leaves a lot of questions about the details. How will these classes operate? When few details are provided, doubt is introduced and the reader will be unsure about the level of planning that the applicant has undertaken to prepare for successful implementation. It is insufficient to tell the reader the "What" without the "How" and you do not want to leave the reader with questions. Unanswered questions will lower your score.

Figure 7 - 2nd Grade Troll Safety Class

The narrative below gives the reader a more fulsome understanding of how the adult troll safety education classes will be implemented. The reader can see that the village knows what needs to be done to implement the classes because the grant presents a detailed plan for how to implement the activity.

Adult Troll Safety Education

Certified troll safety instructors from Manchester—where trolls are common—will be contracted to provide weekly adult classes in the common room of the community building. The shire council has agreed to provide funding for these teachers as an in-kind contribution to the program. Classes and materials shall be provided free of charge for all adults on the island.

The 12-week course comprises three hours class time per week, a total of 36 hours of education. The course shall be repeated four times during the project year. Each class will end with an exam which enables adults to earn their Class A Troll Safety Certificate. Childcare shall be provided by members of the volunteer troll patrol in the adjoining village school. This ensures that all adults may participate without worry that their children are unsupervised and in danger of stewing.

The standard adult RSTA curriculum covers 11 key topics of troll safety in 12 sessions. The session topics include:

1. Troll Basics
2. Trolls in History
3. Special Session on Cotswolds Trolls
4. Troll Habitats
5. Troll Feeding
6. Raising Troll-Safe Children
7. Troll Repellants and Home Protection
8. Troll Protection: Trolls Are People, Too!
9. Special Troll Topics
10. Trolls in Politics (2 sessions)
11. Safeguarding Livestock and Property
12. Troll Safety Exam

Research Base

Research is most frequently cited in the design section because it is important to validate what you are about to do on this quest. Examples of proven strategies in relevant literature are valuable to substantiate your design. The other sections of the narrative tend to be supportive of this section.

It is important to note, it is not that research can't be included anywhere else in the narrative. Quite the opposite is true because anywhere in your proposal where you describe activities for which there is recent, relevant research to cite, you should insert it. One example is the evaluation section that we'll discuss in a later chapter. Perhaps you propose the use of a published test as part of data collection, in this instance you should insert a reference for that test.

In the troll grant, there are a few key bits of fictitious research inserted with footnotes. Be aware that footnotes expand the footer size and that takes up space on the page, so if the RFP allows for a bibliography or end notes that do not count against the page limits, take advantage of that permission and cite references outside the narrative. References are important because the reader wants to know that statements of facts are facts, not the writer's opinion or conjecture.

It is important to remember that grant readers are sometimes, though not always, experienced in the topic of the grant and they are familiar with the research. The reader may know what is good research and what has been disproven, what is recent and what is outdated. So be careful! Just conducting a quick Google search for research articles may turn up references that are going to hurt your grant score, not help it. Do the work of learning all you can about the topic you're writing about within the time constraints. Talk to experts if you have access, ask your client for relevant sources, read the latest issue of the leading journal in the field, conduct more thorough online research, or perhaps even develop a relationship with the state library. California, for example, has an outstanding state library. Your client may be able to give you temporary access to online research databases to which they may subscribe.

The validity of the design is supported by connecting the proposed activities to research-based solutions that are well-documented as effective in other places, and possibly even with similar populations. This kind of research gives the reader confidence that their commitment to the quest is not catch-as-catch-can and that the success of the proposal is not throwing darts in a dark room, but is grounded on previous success.

In the troll grant then, it is important to build the design on current research from the Department of Troll Abatement (a well-recognized source of troll research) and other reliable resources.

Magic (Innovations)

Many stories include elements of magic. Although a grant must be founded on facts and research, you may want to include innovations tailored to address the needs, these features of a proposal can act as a kind of magic to spark the reader's imagination.

But innovations can be a risky element and undermine the perceived validity of the design. I think of an innovation as an untried method, process, or a new project-created material as opposed to a published material, or methods of implementing research-based activities in the same way that is proven effective in the literature. Innovations may not be able to substantiated with research directly. There may also be no direct precedent for what an innovation proposes to do, although perhaps there are tangential relationships that can add strength to the notion that a new idea will work. Innovations are interesting but can be difficult to explain with enough detail to convince the reader within the page limits of a grant narrative. In addition, the qualifications of the key personnel who are tasked to design, plan, and implement the magic must be unquestionable.

There are several keys to successfully including an innovation in a grant narrative:

> 1. ***Never include innovations without the client's approval***. *A "cool" idea can be poorly thought out and impossible to implement, especially when it is a creation of a writer who works outside of the organization.*
>
> 2. ***Always try to connect innovative activities to research***. *You want to convince the reader that the innovation will work as intended and lead to achievement of the objectives.*
>
> 3. ***Ensure that adequate funding is budgeted or provided in-kind to implement the innovation***. *Adequate training must also be planned since an innovation is new, and adequate time must be set aside for planning, revising, tweaking, re-tweaking, and assessing the effectiveness of the innovation.*

Innovation is tricky because successful grants build trust with the reader, so, whenever possible, connect the design magic to research. In doing so, a grant writer can leverage success demonstrated elsewhere to convince the reader that the quest using the same methods can be successful.

Including magical elements in a grant automatically raises questions and tests a reader's trust, so introducing an innovation requires more convincing and more explanation, and it means that no detail is too small to include. This can also mean there simply isn't room to adequately describe the innovation. In these cases, unless the innovation is central to meeting the needs, it would be better to leave it out and suggest to the grantee that they approach the funder after an award is received to see if a modification of the program design and budget to include an innovation would be acceptable.

The troll grant could have included an innovative training program, or an untried innovation such as trying to change the eating behavior of trolls using behavior modification techniques to turn them into docile, non-children-stewing beings. But this may be too innovative and perhaps scoffed at by readers who were troll experts. Such an innovation could raise serious questions for readers about the adequacy of time and money allocated. It is important to remember that the purpose of the funding agency is what the grants are funding, if the stated purpose is not to discover innovative solutions, beware of making that a central activity of your design.

So, you can see that inserting an innovative magic element can undermine the credibility of your design and put your score at risk by losing the reader's trust.

Innovations that address conditions identified in the needs for which there are few research-based solutions are more likely to be accepted by the readers. For example, perhaps a specific reading intervention is proposed that the research showed was effective in raising reading levels when implemented in a daily after-school program. But in your proposal you can't afford to run a daily afterschool program so you're only operating four days a week. In this case, in order to keep up the frequency and intensity of the proposed solution, the students will engage in four teacher-guided sessions and take one lesson home to complete over the Friday—Sunday period when there's not an after-school program. This innovation is not creating something from whole cloth but rather merely responding to real world conditions within which any proposal must operate. In this example, the readers are less likely to object to an innovation.

In summary, a successful design section gives the "HOW" and the "WHAT" of all activities planned. It is vital that your design leaves no important questions in the minds of readers and that it logically leads to the achievement of the goals and objectives. Your story must lead the hero to the solution (or solutions), or the grant will not receive funding and the quest may never get started.

Previous History of Success

Grants are sometimes written to extend existing services to meet the same need on a broader scale or for a new population. A school might write a grant to expand an after-school program, for example. Perhaps the school employs one staff member who can care for 30 children but there is a waiting list of 150 students, so the school wants additional funding to expand. Sometimes a grant is written to meet a need that is similar. Perhaps a school has an after-school reading teacher but low student math scores indicate there's a need for a math teacher too.

An agency may write a grant to expand into an area of need in their community that they are unable to address with existing funds. Perhaps an agency gives adult literacy classes but knows that many adults need financial literacy training as well. An application for an unrelated program is more challenging because the agency must convince the reader that the need exists and that they have the capacity to expand their area of expertise into a new area.

In the case of our troll proposal, the Village of Abbingdon must bring troll experts from outside the Isle of Thatch to assist since nobody on the island has troll expertise. This means the grant must describe the quality of the expertise being brought to bear on the problem. The quality of the plan, the curriculum, the safety measures, all of it must work together to lend expertise to the village elders and convincingly support a successful quest.

Village of Abbingdon Troll Abatement Proposal

Read Program Design section in Appendix C

One thing the design does not do is tell the reader how you will know the hero has achieved the objectives and completed their quest. The next section, the management plan, gives specific information about the who, what, when of the proposed project. The management plan is intended to further clarify implementation of the design and provide a tool for grant management throughout implementation.

Management Plan/Timeline><Subplot

Figure 8 - Mrs. Walter Abernathy on Troll Watch

A detailed management plan is a key piece of evidence grant writers use to prove to readers the quest is feasible because adequate planning was undertaken in preparation of the proposal. A grant may implement many activities to achieve the objectives and, as I've stated before, your goal is to leave no unanswered questions by incorporating as many details as the page limitation allows.

The management plan not only helps your readers understand how you're going to move the situation from the problems stated in the needs section to the desired higher state, but it is also a useful guide for grant activity implementation, which is called grant management. The management plan gives clear direction about the anticipated implementation process. Of course, there will be changes and adjustments as grant activities are implemented and evaluated. It could be that the fisherfolk employed to deliver herring for troll feeding has a boat breakdown and a backup source is needed to satisfy the trolls' hunger before they begin scavenging for third graders. These things happen as a grant is implemented, circumstances change and adjustments have to be made on the spot, a grant narrative represents the best plan possible before the quest begins.

Formats and Content

A standard format for a management plan is a table with a series of columns that lay out a chronological chain of events the hero will follow to implement all activities.

A typical format is represented in the column headers shown below. This format is employed in the troll abatement grant and the example below is part of the management plan for the Abbingdon Village troll abatement grant proposal.

Task	Description	Timeline	Responsibility
Convene the troll planning committee	Weekly meetings to create a plan for troll safety.	Upon Funding	Village Elders
Produce a tender for solicitation of a fisherfolk to deliver freshly caught fish for troll feeding	A licensed and experienced Arbuckle fishing firm will be sought to catch and deliver fish for the troll feeding program.	Upon Funding	Village Elders
Deliver fresh fish	Daily delivery of fish to the feeding trough on the island. A minimum of ten pounds of cod or herring each day per troll.	Within 30 days of funding.	Village Elders / Superintendent / Fisherfolk

Management plan content is straightforward but it does require forward-thinking about what will have to be done, so it is important to collaborate closely with the client on this plan. You want to make it as reality-based and useful for implementation as possible. A management plan outlines all major steps, from hiring staff to conducting activities.

The management plan is an explicit example of a section where you anticipate and answer readers' questions about "HOW" this project will be carried out. The table gives many specific details in an organized, logical way that can resolve many reader's questions before they start asking them. The fewer steps missed in the management plan, the fewer questions that readers will raise, and the greater their trust in your proposal.

For novice grant writers, or anyone who hasn't served as a grant reader, it may be useful to know that grants are often scored by "triads," teams of three people. That was my experience reading federal grants. We were given a copy of all grants assigned to our team and we read one at a time scoring them first in isolation. Then we'd come back together to compare scores and negotiate them if needed. Negotiation of scores was required to assure that all scores were within a certain tolerance level. Perhaps on a scale of one–10 for a section, scores had to be within two points. If they were not, we had to explain our score, defend it, and point out evidence in the narrative the other readers may have missed or misinterpreted, etc. The purpose is to adjust someone's score to bring all scores within the range of tolerance. It is at times a frustrating process, but also can be very illuminating and educating about writing a grant narrative that leaves no questions.

Completing a thorough management plan also enables the writer to ensure the budget includes all major costs. It can point to important items that should be itemized in MOUs with partners helping your client to identify all items that should be named and commitments documented. All of these details tie together to paint a convincing roadmap for the reader that the hero has planned thoroughly, paid attention to detail, and that the quest will succeed.

At this point, you have the reader believing in your quest, you have set forth the problem, set goals and objectives for the quest, and described both in the design and management plan sections how the quest will unfold.

Village of Abbingdon Troll Abatement Grant Proposal

Read the Management Plan section in Appendix C

Sustainability Plan

Sometimes there is another required part of the management plan section called a sustainability plan. This is one of the most unimaginable things grant writers must write about. This section describes why the funding requested won't be needed after the grant term. This may seem counter-intuitive because the hero needs the money and because a fundamental characteristic of grants is that nearly 100% of them are temporary. This section is often included because the funder intends to provide seed funding for a project that finds a solution, creates a program that will find community support by the end of the grant term, makes a capital investment that will last, builds strength and capacity within an organization, a leader, or researcher.

The temporary nature of grant funding means that finding ways to sustain important solutions to the problem is a necessary part of a grant's implementation, especially when a grant addresses a need that won't be completely overcome within the project period. The grant writer must address sustainability with skill and understanding about how capacity is built and what it means. If a grant writer makes the mistake of assuming the only factor involved is replacement of grant funds, they'll miss the opportunity to explore effective and low-cost ways to build sustainability.

Here are some ideas about how to build a case for sustainability.

Personnel – A grant design often includes personnel to implement the activities of the grant. Your goal is to build a program design that either includes training existing personnel to take over important grant activities and functions, to learn fundraising methods like grant writing to secure other funds to maintain the grant personnel from other sources if needed, or to demonstrate that the mission of the grant-funded personnel will be completed by the end of the grant term—or will be assumed by existing personnel—so the grant-funded positions simply won't be needed any longer or are integrated into another budget.

Objective Outcomes – Your objectives can also have sustainability built into them.

Perhaps your design includes training on a specific procedure, curriculum, skill, etc., or perhaps a train-the-trainer model is implemented whereby future training will be provided by existing personnel. In this case you're building sustainability within the existing staff.

Perhaps you build a structure or buy a piece of equipment or a vehicle, in this case the capital expense is covered by the grant and all you need to do is demonstrate that sustained maintenance is assured.

Perhaps an objective is to change the way something gets done so you'll modify a policy, create a new regulation, upgrade a process, or install a new stakeholder-based governance structure, these are all sustainable changes that don't necessarily require an ongoing budget.

Perhaps there are collaborative partnerships established through the grant activities, this too builds sustainability for the project objectives and if these partnerships lead to shared costs, all the better for building your sustainability argument.

A good grant writer paints a picture of sustainability, and the vision is aspirational but must also be realistic. Sustainability is made believable when it is integral to your program design. So, keep sustainability in mind as you write goals, objectives, and activities.

Sustainability is achieved by capacity building. As we've established, this is not always only about finding alternative funds to replace the grant. This is certainly a central concern where it is obvious that a grant's funds are a sort of start-up to address needs that are unlikely to be resolved during the grant term.

Capacity is built in many ways within the troll abatement grant so that minimal ongoing funding can keep the village children safe from trolls after the project year.

> **First** – *A bridge will be constructed to provide trolls with adequate habitat and access to fish. This is capacity within the environment of the island.*

> **Second** – *All villagers, adults and children, will complete a course of troll safety. This knowledge does not disappear at the end of the project. Then there is the grant-purchased curriculum and the training of teachers in the school to provide the training. This builds capacity within existing staff.*

> **Third** – *A system for troll safety will be installed and will require little maintenance after initial costs of installation are paid from grant funds. The system is manned by volunteers from the village and these volunteers will be thoroughly trained by the paid officers during the project year. This builds capacity within the preparedness of the village and within its residents.*

This level of capacity built into the project will make the readers feel confident that the troll abatement program will continue and protect the village for many years to come. Many grants are given to solve a long-term problem with short-term funding. Funders want to believe that their investment has a realistic chance to make that happen.

Village of Abbingdon Troll Abatement Proposal

Read the Sustainability Plan in Appendix C

Grant projects often involve multiple participants, partners, and collaborators; these stakeholders can add strength to the project design and ultimate success of the project, they also support sustainability. In the next section, we will look at how to write about these important players in your quest.

Partnerships and Collaborations

Borrowing expertise can be accomplished through agreements with other agencies, or contracts with bona fide consultants who bring needed experience and knowledge. Remember that a "letter of support" is not strong documentation of a partnership. A memorandum of understanding (MOU) is stronger documentation of a partnership because it details what each partner commits to do. It is wise to include the dollar value of the contributions whenever possible. Too many novice grant writers believe that collecting 25 letters of support to append will sway the readers, but letters of support probably won't be read at all. It takes advance planning and collaboration to put together MOUs between partners in support of a grant proposal while a letter of support usually involves nothing more than a phone call or email to obtain. An applicant's ability to refer to MOUs created for the proposal can pay off handsomely in the scoring because the reader is confident that the hero is not going it alone; rather, there is a team commitment to the quest.

The Village of Abbingdon proposes to bring in outside expertise to support the quest in the form of publishers of curriculum, adult educators, experienced safety officers, an experienced superintendent, all supported and guided by the village elders.

Describe documentation of support for your project in terms of written and signed agreements, and by including concise descriptions of qualifications, either that of actual predesignated experts or prerequisites for a potential new staff member in the hero section.

In conclusion, the readers must be confident that the hero, or the hero *and* their support team, is able to carry out the quest. They should be impressed, if not in admiration of the qualifications of the hero. Any questions about the capabilities of the hero can result in dragging down your score. So, describe your hero as fully as the page limits will allow. Remember that our hero's resume must be strong, the partners or consultants must contribute vital skills or resources and hopefully gravitas, and the description of the qualifications for staff to be hired must be comprehensive and well-thought-out.

Village of Abbingdon Troll Abatement Proposal

Read Partnerships and Collaborations section in
Appendix C

One thing the design and management plan sections do not do is tell the reader how you will know the hero has achieved the objectives of the quest. How do you propose to measure success? That will be covered in the next section, evaluation, which describes the means and methods by which you will test the quality of the design implementation and the level of achievement of the quest.

Evaluation Plan><Beneficiaries

In the evaluation section, the grant writer presents a detailed plan to measure, analyze, and assess the success of grant activities toward achieving the quest objectives.

The evaluation design is derived from the objectives and the management plan. As we discussed in the "Goals and Objectives" chapter, grant objectives need to be written as SMART objectives. And recall that the M stands for...measurable! The measurements defined in the objectives lay out the primary roadmap to grant program outcome assessment.

It is most effective to present the evaluation design in a table that outlines timelines, assessments, responsibilities, and processes for using evaluation data to inform program implementation and management.

Evaluation activities are usually divided into two categories, outcome assessment and process assessment. Outcome evaluation is data-driven and these data assess the degree to which something changed as a result of grant activities, and whether the change achieved the objectives proposed. Process evaluation focuses on assessing the processes put into place to implement the grant program. Process evaluation is usually assessed with anecdotal information, direct observations, sometimes using established tools or focus groups of participants or community stakeholders. The purpose is to get a clear picture of grant implementation and what barriers are encountered. Most of the processes that need to be evaluated are written into the management plan so it is a good tool for guiding process evaluation.

Outcome Evaluation

Objectives state the outcomes in measurable terms so if the objectives are written properly to address the needs, the evaluation design measures how well the grant resolved the needs identified. Outcome assessment assesses the participants' state of bliss—the extent to which participants' needs were met by the grant activities. The evaluation plan sets forth a plan to collect data, including identification of specific assessments, surveys, observations and analysis that help the program managers and stakeholders determine the extent to which the beneficiaries have reached a higher state, free from the needs described. In the troll grant, the extent to which the villagers and their children are free from the threat of trolls is measured by the reduction in troll sightings and the successful relocation of the trolls.

Anyone who has managed complex projects knows that implementation is difficult and it almost never goes exactly as planned. This is why evaluation is so important and describing a detailed process for collecting and using evaluation data further cements trust with the reader. A strong evaluation plan allows the reader to say to themselves, "They not only know what the problems are and how to correct them, they also know how to measure whether they've achieved the quest!"

Measurable outcomes detailed in the troll grant objectives are:

- A bridge will be completed in 12 months;
- 200 adults will complete troll safety training;
- All school children will achieve A or B troll safety levels;
- Zero children will be stewed through deployment of an extensive troll safety plan.

Process Evaluation

Measuring the outcomes, or the achievement of the higher state, is important, but a good evaluation design also includes methods to review and assess the success of the design *implementation*. Process evaluation includes activities wherein the grant staff and often stakeholders review information, both anecdotal and data, to assess the progress being made by the grant staff and project partners in implementation of the grant activities. In our troll grant, the lord mayor, project superintendent, village elders and collaborative partners meet monthly throughout the project to engage in process evaluation.

Process assessments indicate whether implementation is going as planned and whether barriers exist that must be addressed in order for the quest to be successful and outcomes achieved. It is common to establish an evaluation team for large grants that includes the project leadership, representatives from stakeholder groups and partnerships. The evaluation team meets on a regular schedule and receives reports from the grant team on how implementation is progressing according to the management plan timelines, what barriers are being encountered and to receive feedback and assistance from the evaluation team to resolve any difficulties. If there is an evaluation consultant on a grant project, that person may also provide input to the evaluation team through direct observation and by conducting focus groups. Process evaluation is an important management tool in implementing a successful grant program.

What is the Higher State?

The objective outcomes describe the end of the quest and a higher state. In the troll grant the higher state is one of safety from trolls. The grant activities lead the villagers out of the dangerous state of misfortune and the trolls to a better life. The evaluation section explains how data on the grant activities are collected, analyzed, and reported for the purpose of validating that the higher state has been achieved and by that achievement the needs are resolved.

The program evaluation, like the project design section, describes activities that are necessary for the hero to go on the quest and to measure its success.

Village of Abbingdon Troll Abatement Proposal

Read the Evaluation section in
Appendix C

What the grant writer has to do next is show the readers how the grant award will be budgeted to support the quest which we will discuss in the next chapter, "Budget, Funding & Sustainability."

Budget, Funding &Sustainability><Magic Talisman

The hero of a fictional story often needs something magical, a talisman, to complete their quest. This talisman is often obtained from what is referred to by Joseph Campbell as a threshold guardian who requires that the hero pass a test before they're awarded the magic talisman, which is necessary to complete their journey.

Figure 9 - Wisty Wedlock

Threshold guardians and a magic talisman are perfect analogs for grant competitions. The readers are threshold guardians and the talisman is the check that funds your hero's budget. In grant competitions, the writer must pass a test by writing a fundable grant. Passing this test, the hero is granted the talisman and the quest can begin.

In my experience as a grant reader, I found that examining the budget before reading the grant told me a lot about the real purpose of the application narrative. I learned where the money would be spent, what personnel would be hired, what equipment was needed, and what consultants might be employed. Reviewing the budget first also gave me a sense of the care with which the application was prepared. I checked all the math involved with a calculator and I sometimes got a negative first impression when I found errors in math within the budget, it told me a story of carelessness that raised questions about the ability of the hero to carry out the quest.

Sometimes the budget included items that didn't fit the quest. I was left with serious questions about the needs when items were included that were not necessary to achieve the objectives. For example, an item that frequently appeared in grants was excessive amounts of technology when the solutions to the needs were not technology-based. It became obvious that the grant budget was being improperly leveraged to gain needed technology. This type of budgeting most often ruins a grant's chance of winning an award, no matter how great the needs addressed were or how great the need was for modernizing their computers. To totally misquote attorney Johnnie Cochran, "If the line item doesn't fit, get rid of it!"

A budget is one of the last parts of the grant developed because until the entire program is planned, it's hard to decide where the money would best be used to support the goals. Sometimes grant writers miss important items that need to be in the budget. It would be like the troll abatement grant neglecting to include money for the fisherfolk contractor to feed the trolls during the year of construction. It is a good idea when writing the grant narrative to highlight the text of budget items with green so when the budget is built those highlighted items are easy to locate in the narrative. Don't forget to take out the highlights later!

It is bad enough when a budget omission causes a grant not to be funded, but it can be even worse if the error also slips by the readers. The grant might be funded, but the quest could stall out because the village did not have enough money in the budget to pay for fish to feed the trolls! Worse yet, the grant writer who builds an inadequate budget could end up being handed over to the trolls for stewing!

Figure 10 - Ox

Village of Abbingdon Troll Abatement Proposal

Review the Budget and Budget Narrative in Appendix C

Budgets can be tricky to put together. Whenever possible, even if it isn't a requirement, it's a good idea to add an in-kind budget and in-kind budget narrative to show what other resources, internal or external, will be leveraged to support the success of the quest. Of course, if the RFA explicitly limits the page count for the budget and narrative, it may not be possible to do so. Yes, we are beating this drum again, remember the cardinal rule of grant writing.

Don't be a troll - always follow the instructions in the RFA.

One last bit of advice for building a budget is to do the math correctly, check it, then check it again. Use an Excel spreadsheet to build your budget so calculations are done automatically—but also make sure your formulas are correct! Then when you paste it into a Word document, get out that calculator and make sure it is perfect. You want to be confident that you didn't make any mathematical errors because one day I may be your reader!

The next important part of your grant is the budget narrative. In this section you will provide details for each line item to validate the amounts requested and to expand on the narrative with details you otherwise don't have room to include in the narrative.

Budget Narrative

Veteran grant writers know that the budget narrative is a terrific tool for extending the grant narrative. This is where you can add finer detail because the budget narrative is often not part of the narrative page limit. A budget narrative enables a skilled writer to insert key details about expenditures there is no room to include within the page-restricted narrative.

At the same time, good writers also know that information absolutely vital to success must be written into the narrative and not buried in the budget narrative. Remember that if it isn't scored, readers are not necessarily required to read it and since the budget narrative is customarily outside the page limit, it is often excluded from the scored narrative.

So to be clear, it is not that you should write project details into the budget narrative instead of within the project design section; rather, add "nice to know" details that would reinforce the confidence of a thorough grant reader.

For example, if you're hiring a project superintendent, you will be able to describe this to some extent in the narrative, but perhaps you won't have room for a detailed list of duties and responsibilities. You may not want to put that level of detail in the narrative anyway, because it's unnecessary and would bog down the flow. In the budget narrative, however, these details can be appropriate and meaningful, and lend credibility to the level of planning and understanding of the function and necessity of the position to the quest.

The budget narrative line items are organized in the same order as the budget detail. It must include all of the same line items and contain a detailed explanation for each of them. If a number of pounds of herring are to be caught and supplied for troll feeding, then the budget narrative should specify the amount being offered per pound and any additional amounts included in the total, such as fuel surcharges for the boats, etc. Careful readers want to see where the money will be spent and if the amounts are reasonable and well-documented.

A good grant writer knows how to build a little reserve into the budget without it being noticeable.

> *For example, if a position is to be hired, it is always wise to budget that position at the top salary. If the person hired is contracted at less than the top salary, there is a little extra in the budget to buy extra herring. But if the person is hired at the top salary, the hero doesn't need to scrimp elsewhere in the budget to make ends meet. Also, in a multiyear grant, it is wise to include the salary for each year of the grant and include step increases or other salary adjustments that are known or reasonably anticipated.*

Appendices include the troll abatement grant application guidelines and instructions, the grant readers' scoring rubric, a full copy of the Village of Abbingdon troll abatement proposal, the end of project evaluation report describing how the grant went (yes, the grant was funded), and a suggested use of a screen writing tool called a "Beat Sheet" to help you plan your next grant story.

Appendices

Appendix A - Application Guidelines and Instructions

Troll Abatement Grant

Commoner Grant Application

The palace crier doth proclaim throughout the kingdom that Her Majesty the Queen in her infinite wisdom and great munificence doth offer and accept applications for this troll abatement grant to preserve the safety and welfare of her loyal subjects.

Applications shall be considered from cities, villages, and bergs* for the purposes described herein.

Grant administration provided by the Duke and Duchess of Arbuckle, Wales

Application Procedures

1. Use the proposal checklist below to ensure that all necessary documents are submitted. Incomplete applications shall not be considered and shall be used as tinder to burn the hovel of the responsible grant writer.

2. Submit one copy of the complete proposal directly to the palace of the Duke of Arbuckle before the palace drawbridge is raised at sundown on the application due date. *(Please note that grant writers who approach the palace after sundown shall be used as target practice by palace archers.)*

Proposal Checklist (do not submit this checklist with the proposal):

	Application
	Copy of the city, village or berg charter
	List of elders
	Project narrative*
	Attachments of up to 10 pages

*Grant writers are warned to follow the narrative outline on the pain of a stretching on the rack.

Commoner Grant Application

Date of Application: _____

Primary Contact Name: _____

Tick Applicable Square:

City ☐   Village ☐   Berg ☐   Hovel ☐   Best Time to Pillage:
_____:_____

Lord Mayor: _____

Scroll Route: _____

Royal Tax ID Number: _____

Shire: _____

Township: _____

Duchy: _____

Nearest Port: _____

Project Name: _____

Purpose of Grant: _____

_____

_____

_____

Beginning and Ending Project Dates: _____

Amount Requested: £_____

Total Project Cost: £_____

Applications must be delivered on or before the palace drawbridge is raised at sunset on 1st March in the year of our Lord, two thousand and fifteen.
(Please take note that applications delivered late are dead applications, as may well be the unfortunate courier.)

Narrative Instructions

Applicants are directed to scrupulously follow all directions contained herein. Structure the proposal to provide all of the following information in the order indicated. *(Failure to follow these instructions or turning in incomplete or late applications may result in an extended stay in the palace dungeon.)*

Formatting Requirements:

a. Use the headings, subheadings, and numbers provided.

b. 1 inch margin on all pages

c. Font size restrictions do not apply to tables and figures; however, if any reader reports using a magnifier to read a proposal, the grant writer will be put on the first ship to Finland, in January and without shoes.

d. Use 12 point Ariel font for all body text.

e. Use 18 point Olde English font for all headings.

f. Page Limit: 20 double-spaced pages.

g. Greasy finger stains shall disqualify the application.

h. Ale stained parchments are equally unacceptable.

i. Use of condensed fonts shall cause the author to be hung by the ankles with thin and fraying thread above the crocodile-infested moat.

Reporting Requirements
A final project report shall be written and submitted upon completion of the grant project to report on the achievement of grant objectives. The report shall be submitted to the Duke and Duchess of Arbuckle not later than July 31, 2016. Interim reports may also be requested.

Narrative Outline

I. The Needs

a. Unavailability of Comprehensive Troll Abatement Services

b. Lack of Troll Habitat

  c. Lack of Alternative Food Sources

  d. Inadequate Troll Safety Education

  e. Lack of Troll Safety Systems

  f. Imminent Troll Migration

 II. About the Organization

III. Quality of Key Personnel

IV. Program Design

   a. Goals and Objectives

   b. Description of Activities

     i. Creation or Restoration of Troll Habitat

     ii. Troll Safety Education

   c. Troll Safety Systems

   d. Experience or Promise of Success

 V. Management Plan

 VI. Sustainability Plan

VII. Partnerships and Collaborations

VIII. Evaluation Plan

 IX. Budget

 X. Budget Narrative

Narrative Instructions

I. The Needs

Describe the need for a troll abatement program in your city, village, or berg. What are the circumstances that led to the troll problem your citizens are experiencing? Include in your discussion information about each of the following points (a–f).

a. Unavailability of Comprehensive Troll abatement Services

b.Lack of Troll Habitat

c.Lack of Alternative Food Sources

d.Inadequate Troll Safety Education

e.Lack of Troll Safety Systems

f. Troll Migration Patterns

II. About the Organization

Describe your organization's history and present state. What is the leadership structure and where you are located? Include any factors that further describe the need for this grant to receive funding.

III. Quality of Key Personnel

Describe the leadership that will supervise implementation of this grant project and the quality and experience of that leadership. Further, describe additional positions to be included in the grant budget that will undertake key responsibilities in the grant project. Include key qualifications and requirements of proposed personnel.

IV. Description of Activities

Describe proposed activities to be implemented through this grant project that will address the needs described. Specifically address items (a–d) listed below in detail and with specificity.

a. Creation or Restoration of Troll Habitat

b. Troll Safety Education

c. Troll Safety Systems

d. Experience or Promise of Success

V. Management Plan

Provide a detailed management plan for all project activities and administrative functions. This plan should include timelines and assign responsibilities to current or proposed grant-funded personnel.

VI. Sustainability Plan

Describe how the grant activities will be continued beyond the grant period to ensure that this troll abatement grant provides safety for the Queen's loyal subjects of your city/village/berg. What funds will be used to pay for project services and personnel when the grant ends? How will project functions be absorbed within existing activities and by existing personnel?

VII. Partnerships and Collaborations

Describe partnerships and collaborations with individuals and/or organizations that will help assure successful grant implementation. Describe the nature of the agreements and attach memoranda of understanding if one has been established.

VIII. Evaluation Plan

Describe the methods, data, timelines, and methods of analysis and reporting for evaluation of the project. The description should include timelines and assign responsibilities.

IX. Budget Detail

A detailed line-item budget for grant expenditures is to be provided. The grant budget should include all items needed to carry out grant activities. The budget must allocate adequate resources to provide reasonable assurance of successful implementation.

X. Budget Narrative

Provide a narrative description of all budget line items that includes adequate detail to enable grant reviewers to assess the reasonableness and adequacy of each item.

Submission Guidelines:

1. Deadline – 1 March, 2015
2. Deliver the application no later than palace drawbridge closure at sunset on the deadline date.
3. One copy of the completed proposal.

Grant Timeline:

1 March, 2015 – Submission deadline

30 March, 2015 – Applications reviewed and scored

1 April, 2015 – Awards announced

1 July, 2015 – Grant funds provided

30 June, 2016 – Final evaluation report and final invoice due

Grant Term:

1 July, 2015–30 June, 2016

Appendix B – Troll Abatement Grant Scoring Rubric

Grants will be scored by triads of readers with expertise in troll abatement. Applications will be ranked and funding will be distributed in order of rank until the funds provided from Her Majesty's treasury are exhausted. If a funded grantee withdraws their application after scoring, funding will be allocated to the next grant in rank. Grant writers whose proposal scores "Ruddy Awful" in all categories of the scoring rubric will be arrested and forced to labor for 10 years in the royal cabbage fields near Bolton.

Score each section and add comments beneath. Add scoring totals in the right column and total at the bottom.				
Reader Name:		Applicant Name:		Date:
Reading Team Leader:		Project Title:		Total Score:
	Brilliant: 4-5 points	Adequate: 2-3 points	Ruddy Awful: 0-1 points	Total
	Score:	Score:	Score:	
Unavailability of comprehensive troll abatement services	Clear and specific description of program needs, types of trolls present and the problems the trolls are creating and who they impact.	Less than clear and specific description of program needs, types of trolls present and the problems the trolls are creating or who they impact.	Wholly inadequate description of program needs, types of trolls present and the problems the trolls are creating or who they impact.	
Comments				
	Brilliant: 4-5 points	Adequate: 2-3 points	Ruddy Awful: 0-1 points	Total
	Score:	Score:	Score:	

Lack of troll habitat	Clearly documented lack of or loss of troll habitat which causes troublesome and/or dangerous troll dislocation.	Muddled numbers about lack of or loss of troll habitat or about the specific causes of troublesome and/or dangerous troll dislocation.	Wholesale confusion about the lack of or loss of troll habitat or about the specific causes of troublesome and/or dangerous troll dislocation.	
Comments				

	Brilliant: 4-5 points	Adequate: 2-3 points	Ruddy Awful: 0-1 points	Total
	Score:	Score:	Score:	
Inadequate troll safety education programs	**Valid and complete data** about the absence of troll safety education programs **_and_** low rates of troll safety certification.	**Partial or invalid data** about the absence of troll safety education programs **_or_** low rates of troll safety certification.	**Hypothetical and unsubstantiated data** about the absence of troll safety education programs **_and_** low rates of troll safety certification.	
Comments				
	Brilliant: 4-5 points	Adequate: 2-3 points	Ruddy Awful: 0-1 points	Total
	Score:	Score:	Score:	
Lack of troll safety systems	**Clearly documented** absence of troll safety systems or research-based evidence that existing systems are	**Partially documented** absence of troll safety systems or research-based evidence that existing systems are	**No understanding of** troll safety systems or research-based evidence that existing systems	

	outdated or in-adequate.	outdated or in-adequate.	are outdated or inadequate.	
Comments				
	Brilliant: 4-5 points	Adequate: 2-3 points	Ruddy Awful: 0-1 points	Total
	Score:	Score:	Score:	
Additional factors	**Complete Documenta-tion** of special factors specific to the applicant which increase the need for troll abatement funding.	**Partial Docu-mentation** of special factors specific to the applicant which increase the need for troll abatement funding.	**No evidence** that special factors specific to the applicant were considered.	
Comments				

Program Design: 25 Points

	Brilliant: 4-5 points	Adequate: 2-3 points	Ruddy Awful: 0-1 points	Total
	Score:	Score:	Score:	
Background	**A clear and concise de-scription** of the location and of the or-ganization that will implement the grant activ-ities.	**Partial and incomplete description** of the location and of the or-ganization that will implement the grant activ-ities.	**Description** of the location and of the or-ganization that will implement the grant activ-ities indicates they neither know where nor who they are.	
Comments				

	Brilliant: 7-8 points	Adequate: 2-6 points	Ruddy Awful: 0-1 points	Total
	Score:	Score:	Score:	
Goals and objectives	The goals and objectives are **clearly linked** to the stated needs. Objectives are **measurable and achievable** and clearly lead to solutions to the needs presented.	**Not all** the goals and objectives are clearly linked to the stated needs. **Some** objectives are **measurable and achievable** and clearly lead to solutions to the needs presented.	**Few of** the goals and objectives are clearly linked to the stated needs. Objectives are not **measurable nor achievable** and clearly lead to disaster.	
Comments				

	Brilliant: 7-8 points	Adequate: 2-6 points	Ruddy Awful: 0-1 points	Total
	Score:	Score:	Score:	
	Brilliant	Adequate	Ruddy Awful	
Activities	**Clear and specific links** can be made from the goals and objectives to each of the activities included. **All activities** are achievable within the project budget and timeline.	**Clear and specific links** can be made from the goals and objectives to **some** of the activities included. **Most activities** are achievable within the project budget and timeline.	**Clear and specific links** cannot be made from the goals and objectives to **any** of the activities included. **None of the activities** are achievable within the project budget and timeline.	
Comments				

	Brilliant: 2 points	Adequate: 1 point	Ruddy Awful: 0 points	Total
	Score:	Score:	Score:	
Experience or promise of success	**Clearly demonstrates** that the applicant organization has the structural and staff strength to successfully complete the proposed activities.	**Questions exist whether the** applicant organization has the structural and staff strength to successfully complete the proposed activities.	**Clearly demonstrates** that the applicant organization should be shuttered, burned to the ground and the leadership fed to trolls.	
Comments				

Program Management: 25 Points

	Brilliant: 9-10 points	Adequate: 2-8 points	Ruddy Awful: 0-1 points	Total
	Score:	Score:	Score:	
Management Plan	The applicant has provided a **thorough, complete, and detailed** management plan which serves as a roadmap to successful implementation.	The applicant has provided a partial or incomplete management plan which serves as a questionable roadmap to possibly successful implementation.	The applicant has provided a thorough, complete, and detailed roadmap to disorganization, wasteful spending, and lack of results.	
Comments				
	Brilliant: 9-10 points	Adequate: 2-8 points	Ruddy Awful: 0-1 points	Total
	Score:	Score:	Score:	

Sustainability	The applicant presents a **well-considered** plan for sustainability that indicates a high degree of planning and consideration of ways to achieve ongoing implementation of the grant's goals beyond the funding period.	The applicant presents an **un-informed plan** for sustainability that indicates a lack of collaboration in both planning and consideration of ways to achieve ongoing implementation of the grant's goals beyond the funding period.	The applicant has no idea what sustainability means, writes only in monosyllabic words, and has no plan to build capacity in any respect.	
Comments				

	Brilliant: 4-5 points	Adequate: 2-3 points	Ruddy Awful: 0-1 points	Total
	Score:	Score:	Score:	
Quality of Key Personnel	**Clear commitment and capability** on the part of local leadership to successfully implement the grant.	**Unclear commitment or questionable capability** on the part of local leadership to successfully implement the grant.	**Unclear commitment and no documented capability** on the part of local leadership to successfully implement the grant. Application personnel demonstrate almost total incompetence.	
Comments				

Program Evaluation: 15 Points

	Brilliant: 14-15 points	Adequate: 5-13 points	Ruddy Awful: 0-4 points	Total
	Score:	Score:	Score:	
Evaluation Plan	The applicant presents a detailed comprehensive evaluation plan using outcome and process assessments that will produce valid and accurate measurements of the achievement of each proposed objective.	The applicant presents an evaluation plan that lacks details, timelines, and responsibilities using outcome and process assessments that are unlikely to produce valid and accurate measurements of the achievement of each proposed objective.	The applicant presents an evaluation plan that cannot even be trusted to measure the unmitigated disaster this proposal will produce if funded.	
Comments				

Program Budget: 10 Points

	Brilliant: 9-10 points	Adequate: 2-8 points	Ruddy Awful: 0-1 points	Total
	Score:	Score:	Score:	
Budget	The budget is detailed and amounts requested are adequate to ensure achievement of all program objectives. All expenditures are clearly connected to program objectives. The budget narrative provides	The budget is detailed but not all amounts requested are adequate to ensure achievement of all program objectives. Connection of line items to program objectives is unclear. The budget narrative is not detailed	The budget is detailed however vagueness would have served it better. The budget narrative confirms that funding this proposal will lead to disgrace and imprisonment for all involved, not to mention	

	clear and convincing explanations for all budget items.	enough to give clear and convincing explanations for all budget items.	a steady diet of coleslaw for the coming ten years.	
Comments				

Appendix C – Village of Abbingdon Troll Abatement Proposal

Village of Abbingdon

Troll Abatement Program

Grant Application

Submitted by the Right Honorable Lord Mayor Adwir Gittins

Commoner Grant Application

Date of Application: 2/10/2015

Primary Contact Name: Lord Mayor Peate Adwr Gittins

Tick Applicable Square:

City ☐   Village X Berg ☐   Hovel ☐   Best Time to Pillage:

08:00 p.m.

Lord Mayor: Peate Adwr Gittins

Scroll Route: CXXIV

Royal Tax ID Number: MCXIX

Shire: Arbuckle

Township: Brecknock

Duchy: Rheged

Nearest Port: Swansea Docks

Project Name: Abbingdon Village Troll Safety Project

Purpose of Grant: The purpose of this proposal is to ensure the safety of the good people of the Village of Abbingdon from displaced Cotswolds trolls through reconstruction of the bridge over the Firth of Forth and implementation of comprehensive troll safety measures.

Beginning and Ending Project Dates: July 1, 2015–June 30, 2016

Amount Requested: £2,391,506

In-kind Contribution = £2,252,100

Total Project Cost: £4,643,606

Abstract

The Problem

Cotswolds trolls on the Isle of Thatch threaten the safety of children and adults who live in the island's Village of Abbingdon. This dire state of misfortune exists due to the dispersal of the troll population into the island's thatch fields after a storm destroyed the bridge across the Firth of Forth that for many years provided the isle's ideal troll habitat.

Goals and Objectives

This grant proposal establishes a comprehensive troll abatement program that addresses three key elements of the Edinburgh protocols for troll abatement, 1. re-establishing troll habitat, 2. provision of troll safety training programs for adults and children, and 3. installing a troll safety system including a troll watch and electronic warning system throughout the village.

Project Goal – The village elders shall provide the residents of Abbingdon and the Shire of Arbuckle with a troll-safe environment.

- Objective 1 – Reconstruct the Firth of Forth bridge and troll fishing platforms within 12 months of grant approval as measured by a completed, safe, and functional structure.

- Objective 2 – Within the project period, provide troll safety certification training for 200 adults with 90% earning a Class A Troll Safety Certificate, as measured by rosters of participants, attendance records, and a list of adults that earned the Empire's Class A Troll Safety Certification.

- Objective 3 – Within the project period, provide troll safety training and curriculum for all school children that results in 90% of all children earning a troll safety rating of A or B as measured by student attendance, lesson plans, and records of children earning the Empire's troll safety ratings of A or B.

- Objective 4 – Create and implement a troll safety program for the Village of Abbingdon that results in zero children being stewed during the project year, to be measured by installation of electronic monitoring and alert systems, agendas and sign-in sheets from planning meetings, and a published troll safety plan.

The Solutions

Measures of success include construction of a new bridge over the Firth of Forth recreating troll habitat, adults and children of the village will earn Class A or B Troll Safety Certificates, and a troll safety program is instituted.

I. The Needs

This proposal is submitted by the Lord Mayor Peate Adwr Gittins on behalf of the good and loyal subjects of the Village of Abbingdon, on the Isle of Thatch, in the Shire of Arbuckle, Wales. This grant funds implementation of a comprehensive program of troll abatement that aligns with Her Royal Majesty's purpose to "preserve the safety and welfare of her loyal subjects." The activities proposed will spare an estimated 120 village children from being stewed by Cotswolds trolls, the most dangerous and voracious trolls in Great Britain. The comprehensive program of troll abatement will be facilitated by our illustrious village elders and led by a grant-funded project superintendent, a yet-to-be-hired expert in troll abatement. The plans are research-based and include reconstruction of the recently destroyed bridge spanning the dangerous waters of the Firth of Forth. This bridge provided safe passage to the mainland for the islanders and commerce, and it was the only source of troll habitat on the island.

The children of Abbingdon are in danger of being stewed. The trolls are an immediate threat to the Village of Abbingdon and its 400 residents, including 250 children who are especially vulnerable because trolls consider them a favored ingredient in troll stew. This danger demands immediate implementation of a comprehensive troll abatement program.

Trolls became a danger on the Isle of Thatch in 2011, when a great storm destroyed the bridge crossing the Firth of Forth. The trolls lived under the bridge and its destruction displaced the entire colony of Cotswolds trolls that had lived peacefully beneath the structure since its construction.

In spite of the grave danger that trolls pose, they are a protected class in Wales and have enjoyed protected status for centuries. Severe penalties may be imposed for causing harm to a troll, so the proposed abatement program maximizes child safety while minimizing any potential harm to trolls.

Troll protection was initiated by royal decree of King Henry II in 1167. The decree banned trolls from attending Oxford University and relocated them to Wales under the protection of the Crown. At that time, the king forbade Englishmen to study in Paris because young men were returning to England with atrocious manners, filthy poodles, elaborate wigs, and revolutionary ideas like baking bread into long sticks or meals with more than one sauce. Removal of the trolls from Oxford opened seats for returning students where they could be molded into proper English gentlemen.

a. Unavailability of Comprehensive Troll Abatement Services

Abbingdon's troll problem is worsened by the complete lack of troll abatement services on the Isle of Thatch. In 1117, the troll abatement program on the island was disbanded entirely, as it was deemed unnecessary after years of peaceful co-existence.

b. Lack of Troll Habitat

As described above, the Isle of Thatch lacks natural troll habitat (caves and crags). The Firth of Forth Bridge provided dark nooks for sleeping and fishing platforms prior to its destruction. Thatch huts are not favored by trolls but huts are their sole option since the bridge was lost.

c. Lack of Alternative Food Sources

Another key gap in troll abatement was caused by loss of the fishing platforms constructed under the bridge. Lacking access to herring, a troll's favored dish, the hungry trolls now wander about the island scavenging for food, putting village children, a troll's second-favorite dish, in grave danger. Trolls also decimated the island's pig population leaving the entire village without a single Easter ham.

d. Inadequate Troll Safety Education Programs

The children of Thatch are at high risk because, according to a survey prepared for this proposal, no current resident of Abbingdon holds a Class A Troll Safety Certificate. By comparison, 89% of residents hold certificates in other Welsh shires where trolls are common (Troll Abatement Status Report, Dept. of Troll Abatement, 2012).

e. Lack of Troll Safety Systems

Neither paid nor volunteer troll watches have been conducted in Abbingdon since the last paid position for troll abatement officers went vacant when Wally Hirshfield retired and moved to Amsterdam to pursue dodgy relationships and grow tulips. According to research by Professor Darlene Terwilliger of Swansea University, "There is a direct correlation between active troll watches and reductions in the rate of child stewing." Dr. Terwilliger describes relevant research in her tome, *23 Troll Stew Recipes and How to Keep Your Children Off the Menu*, the annual stewing rate in communities with trained volunteers alone is <1:1000. When an organized troll watch is combined with electronic methods for troll alerts, the rate of stewing drops even further to a low 1:5500. In communities without a trained volunteer troll watch or electronic methods, however, the ratio is significantly higher at >10:250 per annum. Hence, the children of Abbingdon are in extreme stewing danger without deployment of a comprehensive program of troll abatement.

f. Imminent Troll Migration

Immediately after the bridge over the Firth of Forth was destroyed, two thatch rafts were discovered on the mainland. Six trolls were found, captured, and returned to the isle, but not before they managed to take a class of sixth grade students hostage during an outing to Raglan Castle. To the great relief of the headmaster, one student was only slightly stewed. Happily, the rescued boy was briefly dipped— not tenderized and mashed—so the wee gaffer recovered and is, once again, fully as obnoxious as only a sixth grader is capable of being.

The abundant thatch grown on the island provides ample natural resources for trolls to construct rafts with which to escape the island, but due to the excellent habitat provided by the bridge and the ample herring to be caught in the waters of the Firth of Forth, this was not a concern while the bridge and fishing platforms were in place. After construction of the original bridge, not a single troll escape from the island was recorded; however, the current lack of habitat and the loss of access to fishing resulting from the destruction of the fishing platforms means that the trolls are on the roam and seeking escape to the mainland where it is certain they will terrorize the shire.

II. About the Organization

History of Abbingdon

The Village of Abbingdon was established on the Isle of Thatch in AD 706 by King Peter IX as an outpost for defense of the mainland against Scandinavian Viking pirates. In those early days the only means of crossing to the isle was by boat, a dangerous undertaking even in fine weather owing to strong currents and unforgiving rocks.

In time, the Viking raiders were subdued, peace reigned, and Abbingdon was abandoned soon after. But soon a new threat emerged on the Welsh mainland as the Cotswolds trolls grew in population and terrorized the villages of the Shire of Arbuckle. The trolls ate whole herds of sheep and made attempts to stew entire classes of school children. It was at this time the trolls were sent to Oxford, it was thought a good education could tame them.

As previously discussed, trolls were banished from Oxford and eventually banished to the Island of Thatch by Queen Rosemary of Tyre in AD 820, after her plump and slow-running firstborn son, Prince Reginald, was captured, stewed, and enjoyed with fresh crusty loaves at a troll festival in Swansea.

In response to this tragic event, the shire council drew up an emergency plan to smoke out the trolls, seal off their crags and caves, and force them into the open. The villagers then lured them onto a barge piled high with fresh herring and towed the barge and all of the trolls to a beach on the Isle of Thatch. There the trolls were isolated (as trolls are unable to swim) and the safety of the shire was restored, alas, too late for poor Prince Reginald.

The plan worked to great success and was hailed by the queen as a triumph akin to the elimination of the snakes from Ireland. The Queen was quoted in the *Shire Cryer*, "The Cotswolds trolls shall never again make stew of a member of the royal family." Security and contentment returned to Wales.

In the years before the Firth of Forth Bridge was constructed, and because the Isle of Thatch lacked natural troll habitat such as crags and caves, the trolls built huts out of thatch, but the trolls were uncomfortable and discontented. Occasionally, a more ingenious troll, which is rare indeed, would devise a thatch raft and float across the Firth of Forth to the mainland and terrorize the inhabitants of the shire. The shire council maintained a program of troll abatement so these trolls were quickly discovered, captured, and returned to the island before they could cause harm or establish shelter.

Scope of the Troll Problem

The abatement of the Cotswolds trolls is of particular urgency due to their voracious appetites. A genetic study revealed that Cotswolds trolls are a cross between the strong Yorkshire and the vicious Oxford trolls, combining the strength and aggressiveness of both breeds. This combination makes the hybrid "exceedingly dangerous, possessing a high metabolism that requires these trolls to take up residence nearby to plentiful food resources," (Troll Quarterly, Autumn Issue: 1889).

As the graph below illustrates, from a study conducted by the Office of Troll Abatement in 1896, the number of Cotswolds trolls per square hectare is directly correlated to the numbers of children stewed.

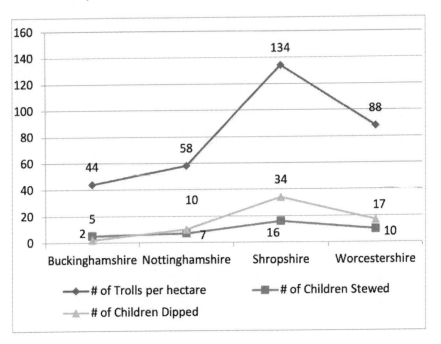

As the population of the Shire of Arbuckle grew over time, the need for sources of thatch increased. Thatch is the most effective and economical roofing material available to keep homes dry. To resolve the shortage, the shire council put a plan in place to establish thatch farms on the Isle of Thatch, owing to the excellent soil and prolonged growing season conducive to farming England's finest thatch (Office of Agriculture, 2002).

Abbingdon was soon re-occupied and thatch farmers were given royal grants to underwrite the establishment of farms. But troll troubles soon emerged. Pigs and sheep began disappearing, and children reported shadows moving on the edges of the football pitch. Four hundred pigs and two hundred sheep disappeared between 1105 and 1115 according to the Shire Council Comprehensive Livestock Report of 1016. The village elders petitioned the shire council for action and it was decided to improve troll habitat to control their movements and monitor their location.

A bridge was soon constructed over the Firth of Forth to connect the island to the mainland. The bridge provided troll habitat and improved access for commerce, and so the colony of thatch farmers thrived. Trolls have a strong preference for dwelling under bridges, preferring bridge habitat even to natural crags and caves (TrollWiki, 2010). A guard house on the mainland end of the bridge ensured no trolls left the island. The project was hailed as a tremendous success, giving easy access to the island's thatch supply and providing the trolls with ample and excellent habitat.

It is commonly known that trolls prefer eating herring to any alternative source of food. In fact, trolls favor fish even over pigs, sheep or stewed third graders.[3] To further enhance the habitat and the safety of Abbingdon children, the village council paid for construction of fishing platforms. This gave trolls access to all the fish they could eat from the waters of the Firth of Forth without fear of falling into the water and sinking.

---

[3] Schleppenpfeifer, A.S., "A Quantitative Study of Troll Flavour Preferences in K-12 Students," Royal Society of Trolls and Polo Players, 1893.

Trolls are well known "to sink like a stone and therefore are well-terrified of water" (Welsh Geographic, December 1965). The platforms were a great success and from 1017–2011; not a single child was stewed and no pigs were taken, and only twelve sheep were reported lost over the 994 year period (In fairness to the trolls, it must be noted that the annual sheep count was unreliable due to persistent somnolence among the census takers).[4]

III. Quality of Key Personnel

Village Elders

The project will be managed by a committee including members of the village elders, community members and the project superintendent. An evaluation contractor will be employed to collect and analyze data, conduct focus group interviews on project implementation effectiveness, make monthly reports to the project committee, and to provide the required final report to the Duke and Duchess of Arbuckle. The committee will be led by Lord Mayor Gittins. The village elders will oversee the project. Elders meet the second Thursday each month in the community room. All meetings are open to the public and delicious snacks are provided by Mrs. Walter Abernathy.

The village elders include: **Mutton Cornwall,** vice chair of the local thatch collaborative; **Lady Elizabeth Overthorn**, good wife of Studs Overthorn, chair of the local thatch collaborative and the power behind the chair as Studs likes to tease; **Sir Edward Tangles**, owner of the local fishing net repair shop and a knight of the Shire of Arbuckle; **Mr. Walter**

---

[4] "Queens' Report on Children Consumed by Trolls" Dept. of Troll Abatement: 2012.

Abernathy, village constable who possesses a girth that honors Mrs. Walter Abernathy's culinary skills; **Pastor Kierkegard Sternly**, pastor of the town chapel and moral compass to the village; **George Reginald Marmalade**, owner of the local pub/jelly shop; and **Lord Mayor Peate Adwr Gittins**, whose father was Earl of Gittinsburg and whose grandfather was Baron of Westchestershire before he was captured in a Viking raid and taken to Scandinavia and never heard from again.

Lord Mayor Gittins will supervise all aspects of the project including employment and training, as needed, of the project staff. Lord Mayor Gittins is a graduate of Eaton with a degree from Cambridge in botanical sciences. He first came to the Isle of Thatch as a royal agricultural consultant to the thatching industry. But his, shall we say, unorthodox approach to thatch propagation is blamed for the thatch blight of 2001. The blight all but ruined the crop and caused the villagers to elect him lord mayor to keep him busy and out of the thatch. The lord mayor is uniquely qualified to lead a troll abatement program as he has encountered, and fled from, per his own accounting (which nobody has cause to doubt the veracity of), every species of troll known to the British Iles.

IV. Program Design

The Village of Abbingdon is the applicant agency for this proposal. The village elders conducted a three-month examination of the needs of the isle with respect to troll abatement and have developed a comprehensive troll safety plan. When implemented, the plan is certain to produce a troll-safe environment on the Isle of Thatch, ensuring the continued safety of the loyal subjects of the Shire of Arbuckle whilst it also gives protection to the trolls.

The plan for troll abatement presented herein is based on the best research available, regarding mitigation of the dangers present in a Cotswolds troll population. The steps outlined below have proven effective in similar regions of Wales with similar populations of trolls. We are utterly confident that our approach will be a complete success and that the adults and children of Abbingdon shall be safeguarded. Furthermore, by restoring troll habitat, the trolls can be relocated successfully from their current unsatisfactory and dangerous habitation among the thatch fields of the Isle of Thatch.

a. Project Goals and Objectives

Project Goal – The village elders shall provide the residents of Abbingdon and the Shire of Arbuckle with a troll-safe environment.

Objective 1 – Recreate troll habitat by reconstructing the Firth of Forth Bridge and troll fishing platforms within 12 months of grant approval as measured by a completed, safe, and functional structure.

Objective 2 – Within the project period, provide troll safety certification training for 200 adults with 90% earning a Class A Troll Safety Certificate, as measured by rosters of participants, attendance records, and a list of adults earning national Class A Troll Safety Certification.

Objective 3 – Within the project period, provide troll safety curriculum and instruction for all school children that results in 90% of all children earning a youth troll safety rating of A or B as measured by student attendance, lesson plans, and records of children earning national youth troll safety ratings of A or B.

Objective 4 – Create and implement a troll safety plan for the Village of Abbingdon that results in zero children stewed during the project year, to be measured by stewing instances, installation of electronic monitoring and alert systems, agendas and sign-in sheets from planning meetings, and a published troll safety plan adopted by the village elders.

b. Description of Activities

A comprehensive program of troll abatement will be deployed by the village elders of Abbingdon. The elders will implement the Edinburgh Protocol[5] for troll abatement that includes the following key components:

- Creation or restoration of troll habitat
- Provision of adequate non-child, non-sheep food sources
- Establishment of troll safety education programs
- Installation of troll safety systems

The Edinburgh Protocol is the worldwide gold standard for troll abatement published in 821 (formally adopted by the United Nations, Committee on Troll Abatement, in 1959). The protocol was written by experts appointed to the then newly-established Royal Society for Troll Abatement (RSTA) through a grant from Queen Rosemary of Tyre. The members of the RSTA included the most renowned group of troll scholars ever assembled. Omar Klinkowikz, the respected,

---

[5] Edinburgh Protocol: A Prescription for Troll Abatement, Royal Society for Troll Abatement, Edinburgh, Scotland, 825 AD.

nine-foot-tall expert on Cotswolds trolls (long rumored to be half Romanian troll himself), was appointed as the first chair of that esteemed body.

i. Creation or Restoration of Troll Habitat

The Firth of Forth Bridge will be reconstructed during the project year by a stonemason to be hired after an open bidding process is conducted. The span will be 3,000 meters long and 10 meters in width. The bridge spans the narrowest point of the Firth of Forth from Crown Point North on the island to The Mumbles west of Swansea—facilitating export of thatch, and providing the islanders safe, easy access to the shire nightlife and shopping.

Stone materials for the bridge are to be quarried locally, thereby protecting the environment and reducing the cost of transport. The bridge will be of Roman stone arch construction with a total of ten arches supporting the span. Solar lamp posts will be installed every 20 meters across the deck and a decorative metal railing shall provide a safety barricade to protect the crossing villagers.

On the underside of each arch (with the exception of the two arches nearest the mainland), ledges will be built to the width of the arches to provide sleeping nooks for trolls.

At the base of each pillar a fishing platform is constructed to provide the trolls with easy access to catch herring, thereby eliminating the need for trolls to forage on the isle.

A guard tower will be constructed at the mainland end of the bridge with a gate that seals the bridge and enables guards to prevent trolls from passing across the bridge onto the mainland.

Structured Interim Feeding Program

Research indicates that, "When fish are readily available, trolls eschew other sources of food even when pigs, sheep, or plump and slow-running children are plentiful."[6] Providing the Cotswolds trolls with a supply of fish during the reconstruction of the Firth of Forth Bridge will ensure that trolls are well-fed and disinclined to pursue alternate food sources.

A temporary feeding trough will be constructed under a stone arch, of the same design and construction as the new bridge, near the edge of the thatch fields where the trolls currently live. A fishing contractor shall be engaged to deliver fresh fish to the trough daily. The fish shall be poured into the trough an hour before sunset when the trolls become most active. Feeding will continue daily until the bridge is completed and the trolls are relocated to the arches where they can once again hang fishing strings from their long, furry toes to feed themselves. At this time, the fishing trough shall be dismantled, and the stone arch shall be cleansed and repurposed to serve the community park for special events and weddings.

---

[6] Jaberwocky, M. *Trolls of Wales: A Comprehensive Analysis of Feeding Habits.* Crown Publishers, London, 2010.

ii. Troll Safety Education

Isle of Thatch residents became complacent about troll safety during the 900+ years of peaceful coexistence. This proposal re-establishes troll safety programs for adults and children using research-based curriculum materials. Adult classes will be provided in the community center whilst children will have troll safety integrated into their standard curricula to be instructed during their school day.

Adult Troll Safety Education

Certified troll safety instructors from Manchester—where trolls are common—will be contracted to provide weekly adult classes in the common room of the community building. The village and the shire council entered into a memorandum of understanding (MOU) wherein the council agreed to underwrite the cost of the teachers as an in-kind contribution to the program. Troll safety classes and materials are to be provided free of charge for all adults on the island.

The 12-week course comprises three hours class time per week, a total of 36 hours of education. The course shall be repeated four times during the project year. Each class will end with an exam which enables adults to earn their Class A Troll Safety Certificate. Child care shall be provided by members of the volunteer troll watch in the adjoining village school. This ensures that all adults may participate without worry that their children are unsupervised and in danger of stewing.

The standard adult RSTA curriculum covers 11 key topics of troll safety in 12 sessions. The session topics include:

1. Troll Basics
2. Trolls in History
3. Special Session on Cotswolds Trolls
4. Troll Habitats
5. Troll Feeding
6. Raising Troll-Safe Children
7. Troll Repellants and Home Protection
8. Troll Protection: Trolls Are People, Too!
9. Special Troll Topics
10. Trolls in Politics (2 sessions)
11. Safeguarding Livestock and Property
12. Troll Safety Exam

Child Troll Safety Education

All children attending the Abbingdon Comprehensive School will participate in eight hours of troll safety education. The objective is for all children to achieve an A or B troll safety rating on the national troll safety exam. Children who score a mark of C or worse shall be sent to remedial troll lessons with a personal tutor paid for through project funding.

The curriculum chosen for this program is *Trolls Are Bad for You and Me*, published by the Royal Troll Safety Council of Aberdeen. The curriculum is a combination of workbooks and online videos which are combined to deliver a rich multimedia curriculum. The curriculum equips children to guard their safety in a troll-challenged environment.

The topics covered in this high-quality curriculum include:

1. How to Recognize a Troll
2. Life Cycle of a Troll
3. How to Avoid and Escape Trolls
4. Troll Dos and Don'ts
5. Safety in the Neighborhood
6. Don't Feed the Trolls
7. What to Do When Trolls are Lurking
8. Troll Review and Exam

Teachers will receive two hours of in-service, train-the-trainer training delivered by certified trainers from the Royal Troll Safety Council of Aberdeen on how to effectively implement the curriculum. Each teacher will receive a complete classroom set of books and online access to student activities.

c. Troll Safety Systems

An important element of keeping all Abbingdon residents safe, especially the children, is establishment of a system of troll alerts. At present, the sole troll alert system is haphazard; it consists of Mrs. Walter Abernathy sitting on her stoop in a rocker. She screams bloody murder to alert the villagers whilst banging a wooden spoon on a pot bottom whenever she spies a troll. Mrs. Abernathy has a fine set of lungs for the purpose but wears out over the course of the week. The poor dear tends to nod off in her rocker and snore with such energy that the cacophony is sometimes mistaken for an alert. Needless to say, this proposal will bring significant improvements to the island's alert system…and allow dear Mrs. Abernathy some well-deserved rest.

A number of components are necessary to enact an effective program of troll alerts. These include:

- **Official troll watch patrols** are to be established around the perimeter of the village. Three officers will be employed with project funds and shall provide round-the-clock patrols in three, eight-hour shifts. A volunteer Troll Safety Corps shall supplement the paid officers as described in more detail below.

- An **alert bell** shall be installed in the center of town at the top of the three-meter pole used annually in the May Day celebrations (and illicitly on the sad occasion that Olivia Rosebud practiced for a pole dancing audition publicly, thereby interrupting the thatch harvest festival and sparking a month-long series of sermons on sober living by Pastor Kierkegaard Sternly [at the insistence of his good wife, known affectionately in the village as "Sister Stern"]) The bell shall be electronic and so it may be remotely activated by the troll watch on duty, or by electronic sensor (see details on the sensor below).

- A **volunteer troll watch corps** will be recruited from among the villagers. A minimum of 32 adults will be recruited and trained to high British military standards to assist in troll abatement patrols, supervise troll feeding, and maintain troll alert equipment. The three paid officers hired during the project year will establish the troll watch and provide ongoing training and supervision.

- A series of electronic **troll sensors** will be installed at key access points to the village. These sensors are infra-red and able to discern the uniquely low body temperature of trolls from that of human and animal body temperatures. The sensors feed into an advanced computerized troll alert system that auto-dials warnings to all villager's phones, it sounds the bell, and it notifies the troll watch of the location of the incursion.

d. Experience or Promise of Success

This troll abatement proposal is based on a comprehensive plan developed using the Edinburgh Protocol as described above. This protocol is well-validated in numerous research studies (M. Python AD 904; Bean and Thatcher AD 997; Cooper, Fenswick and Hatfield 1506; Fezziwig, Marley, et al, 2003).

The project budget shall pay for a full-time superintendent position to manage the project (under the direction of our good lord mayor), oversee the budget, and ensure that all objectives and management plan benchmarks are met. Fidelity to the Edinburgh Protocol is a primary responsibility of the superintendent.

The qualifications for this position shall include:

1) Recent experience in a leadership position within a troll abatement program located geographically in an active troll region.

2) Experience in troll management.

3) Knowledge of troll abatement principles and feeding practices.

4) Superior communication skills and experience working in collaborative relationships.

5) Possess a current troll safety certificate—master trainer level.

6) Experience in construction management is preferred.

V. Management Plan

Chain of Command

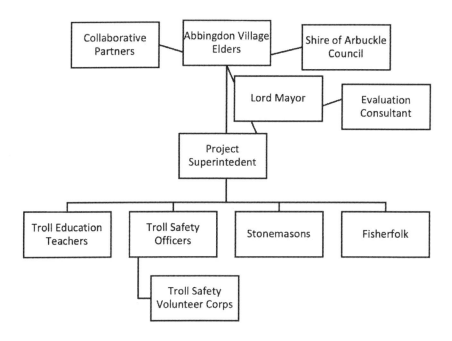

Detailed Management Plan with Timeline

Task	Description	Timeline	Responsibility
Convene the Project Planning Committee	Weekly meetings to create a plan for troll safety.	Upon Funding	Village Elders
Solicit proposals from evaluation consultants.	Selection of a qualified candidate will be informed by the RSTA preferred list of troll abatement evaluation consultants.	Upon Funding	Village Elders
Produce a tender for solicitation of a fisherfolk to deliver freshly caught fish for troll feeding.	A licensed and experienced Arbuckle fishing firm will be sought to catch and deliver fish for the troll feeding program.	Upon Funding	Village Elders

Deliver fresh fish.	Daily delivery of fish to the feeding trough on the island. A minimum of ten pounds of cod or herring each day per troll.	Within 30 days of funding.	Village Elders, Superintendent and Fisherfolk
Recruit a volunteer corps and provide training.	Employ Mrs. Abernathy to staff a table outside the school each afternoon and outside the church on Sundays to recruit.	Upon Funding	Mrs. Abernathy
Post advertisements for a project superintendent and troll safety officers.	Purchase ads in the Arbuckle Crier and post them in local pubs.	Upon Funding	Village Elders
Create a tender to solicit bids from stonemasons for the bridge construction.	Create engineered plans and specifications sheets for the bridge.	30 days from date of funding.	Village Elders
Post advertisements for troll Safety teachers for adult classes.	Conduct recruitment, interviews, background checks (troll screening), and process for employment.	Hire within 30 days of funding.	Village Elders
Organize adult troll safety classes.	Create and post notices, take enrollment, reserve space, organize child care, facilitate sessions.	Within 60 days of funding.	Village Elders and Troll Safety Teachers
Order school-age troll safety curriculum.	Gather enrollment data from the school and order supplies.	Upon Funding	School Headmaster
Provide training for teachers on proper implementation of troll safety curriculum.	Schedule an in-service day for teachers to be trained and certified to deliver troll Safety curriculum.	Within 30 days of funding.	School Headmaster
Schedule administration of national troll exams	Organize proctors and schedule a testing period for adults and children.	To be scheduled within ten days of completion of each adult class	Adult Teachers and School Headmaster

for adults and children.		session and at the end of the first school term.	
Creation of a tender for bids to install an alert bell and troll sensors.	The successful company will provide state-of-the-art troll sensors and alarm systems with remote activation capabilities.	Within 30 days of funding.	Village Elders and Superintendent

VI. Sustainability Plan

The comprehensive system of troll abatement will continue to protect the loyal subjects of Abbingdon beyond the funding period through incorporation of a variety of components that build capacity within the village.

- **New Bridge** – The reconstructed Firth of Forth Bridge will provide long-lasting troll habitat (sleeping nooks) and fishing platforms that give trolls access to their preferred food source.

- **Troll Alert System** – It is anticipated that the trolls will be sufficiently content in the new habitat that they will pose no serious risk to the children of Abbingdon; so, a volunteer corps will be sufficient protection against unwanted consumption of children. But the Lord Mayor Gittins will also engage village elders in discussions as to incorporation of the cost of one or all of the paid troll watch officer positions as part of the village budget. A combination of volunteers and the electronic monitoring devices will continue to provide safety to the village beyond the funding period. At the end of the project period, the village elders will take over volunteer troll watch training and scheduling and the paid officers will be released at the end of their contract year, unless the village budget assumes this cost.

- **Adult Troll Education** – The village elders have committed (see memoranda of understanding [MOU] attached) to fund continuing troll safety education annually for all adults.

- **Student Troll Education** – The headmaster shall continue to ensure that troll safety curriculum is taught during the school each year and that students continue to earn national certificates in troll safety (see Abbingdon school MOU attached).

VII. Partnerships and Collaborations

This proposal was developed with the input and expert guidance of a collaborative group comprised of highly qualified partners. Each of these partners has agreed to provide specific assistance in the successful implementation of this proposal.

Royal Society for Troll Abatement (RSTA) – Established in AD 821 by Queen Rosemary in memory of the most unfortunate Prince Reginald. The RTSA has agreed to provide a matching grant in support of the education components of the grant in the amount of £ 20,000.

The Council of the Shire of Arbuckle – The council provides matching funds including £ 2,000,000 for half the cost of the bridge, supporting the wages and benefits for the gatekeepers staffing the bridge guard house (£ 80,000 per year), and maintenance of the entire span in perpetuity (approx. £ 20,000 per year). The council further agreed to expedite the permitting process for the construction and waive all permit fees so that all of the planned activities may be completed within the project year at lower expense.

Abbingdon Comprehensive School – Kilted Headmaster Clyde Wallace participated on the planning team for this proposal and has advised the engagement of students, the selection and deployment of curriculum, and approved use of the school lunch room for troll safety team planning meetings as needed, and for child care during adult troll safety classes.

Cotswolds Troll Abatement Curriculum for Adults, 64th Edition – Alistair Oystermouth Publishers – The publisher agreed to provide a 50% discount on all materials purchased through the project for adult troll safety education on the Isle of Thatch.

The Royal Troll Safety Council of Aberdeen – The council granted full access to its curriculum and troll abatement web site resources for all children on the Isle of Thatch during the project year. Project funding will pay for travel, lodging, and per diem for council instructors to conduct training for the teachers at Abbingdon Comprehensive School.

VIII. Evaluation Plan

The Abbingdon village elders have convened annually in May since the village was inhabited to assess the village status, agricultural success, general budgetary needs, and to celebrate the blessings of spring. Among the tasks completed during this meeting are establishment of the annual budget for the village expenses and gathering of testimony from residents about pressing agricultural issues for consideration. This year the elders will add to the agenda an assessment of the troll abatement program.

Throughout the project year, a committee of village residents, select village elders and the superintendent will meet with the lord mayor, on a monthly basis to review the management plan, to assess achievement of grant benchmarks, and to provide assistance in overcoming obstacles. The meetings shall be facilitated by the project superintendent who shall employ Mrs. Walter Abernathy to provide tea, crumpets, scones, and her transcendent pickled herring. Mrs. Abernathy is recognized across the isle as an excellent hostess and the finest chef. Her warm hospitality and culinary talents will help to maintain the focus, good humor and congeniality of all in attendance.

Evaluation Plan

1. The rebuilding of the Firth of Forth Bridge shall be assessed in four phases as described above in the management plan timelines. The successful relocation of the trolls to this habitat shall be measured by a reduction in the number of troll sensor alerts which should progress commencing with the completion of the bridge decking as outlined in the construction schedule to be provided by the contracted firm.

2. Troll feeding records shall include the tons of fish delivered, the number of trolls recorded feeding from the trough weekly, and the number of pigs or sheep gone missing, and children stewed (or dipped) over the project year.

3. Troll safety education will be measured by rosters of adults and children who attended, the Level A Troll Safety Certificates earned by adults, and the A and B levels achieved by the children.

4. Troll safety program success will be assessed by records of patrols, numbers of volunteers, and by a pre-post reduction in the number of troll alerts in the village.

Evaluation Management Plan

Tasks	Timeline	Responsibility
Collect pre troll relocation and post relocation sensor alert data and provide reports to project management committee (committee).	Monthly	Lord Mayor, Evaluation Consultant, and Committee
Maintain invoice records for herring purchased.	Weekly	Committee
Troll watch will observe feeding to record the number of trolls present.	Daily	Troll Watch
Conduct pig and sheep census to monitor the population.	Monthly	Farmers and Committee
Collect data on cases of stewing and dipping.	Monthly	Lord Mayor and Secretary of Village Health
Troll safety training records including attendance and test data.	Quarterly	Committee and Troll Safety Instructors
Troll safety records including roster of troll watch, training records, schedules of patrols and feeding observations, records of troll alerts.	Monthly	Troll Watch and Committee
Write and submit the required final report to the Duke and Duchess of Arbuckle.	June 2016	Evaluation Consultant

IX. Budget

Line Item	Budget Amounts	In Kind Amounts
Personnel		
Project Management		£50,000
Project Superintendent	£50,000	
Troll Safety Officers	£40,000	
Volunteer Troll Watch		£46,080
Gatekeepers		£80,000
Fringe Benefits		
25% of all salary amounts.	£22,500	£44,020
Materials and Supplies		
Troll Safety Curriculum - Adult	£750	
Troll Safety Curriculum - Children	£1000	
Food for adult education classes and childcare.	£5,400	
Equipment		
Troll Alert System	£15,000	
Other		
Facilities & equipment for adult education.		£12,000
Contractual		
Fishing contract for troll feeding.	£43,800	
Stonemasons for bridge construction.	£2,000,000	£2,000,000
Adult Troll Safety Teachers		£7,500
Evaluation Contractor	£50,000	
Bridge Maintenance		£20,000
Indirect Costs		
7%	£163,056	
Total		
	£2,391,506	£2,252,100

X. Budget Narrative

Line Item	Narrative
Personnel	
Project Superintendent	A full time project superintendent to develop the tenders, conduct the bidding process, manage contracts, and oversee the work of the contractors (stonemasons and fisherfolk), to hire and supervise the troll safety officers, communicate with the village elders and make formal reports about grant activities throughout the project period, recruit, hire, and coordinate with adult troll Safety instructors, order curriculum materials for adults and children, assist with training of the volunteer troll watch, process financial paperwork, maintain records, develop reports on grant accomplishments, and communicate with the media about project accomplishments.
Troll Safety Officers	Three full-time, licensed troll safety officers that will work eight-hour shifts daily to patrol the village and protect the safety of the village residents against intrusion by trolls as well as provide training to volunteer corps and coordinate with volunteers to assist in patrol and alarms.
Fringe Benefits	
25% of all salary amounts.	Includes health, welfare, and taxes according to the requirements of the village employment agreement.
Materials and Supplies	
Troll Safety Curriculum – Adult	Purchase of 150 copies (1 per village adult) of the RSTA Troll Safety Curriculum for Adults @5/copy x £150£ = £750
Troll Safety Curriculum – Children	Purchase of 200 copies (50 of the children are not yet old enough to be in school) of *Trolls Are Bad for You and Me* the RSTA Curriculum @5/copy x 200 = £1,000
Food for adult education classes and childcare.	A nutritious snack for all participants of the adult troll safety classes @£3 per participant x 12 days x 150 participants = 5,000£
Equipment	
Troll Alert System	Purchase and installation of an electronic troll alert system such as the Troll Screecher 2000™ or similar.
Other	
Facilities & equipment for adult education.	All facilities and equipment for troll education courses are provided as an in-kind contribution.

Contractual	
Fishing contract for troll feeding.	Provide funds to employ a local fisherfolk to catch and deliver sufficient herring to the project-provided feeding trough on a daily basis throughout the project period.
Stonemasons for bridge construction.	Provides funds to contract with a licensed royal stone contractor to provide all materials, labor, engineering, geological surveys, and permitting processes to construct a new bridge across the Firth of Forth including fishing platforms and a stone arch and trough for troll feeding.
Adult Troll Safety Teachers	The shire council will provide teachers to the village for four courses throughout the year.
Evaluation Consultant	A consultant will be chosen after proposals are solicited. The successful consultant will be chosen from among those applicants listed as qualified troll abatement program evaluators on the RSTA-approved list.
Indirect Costs	
7%	Indirect costs include all items not directly attributable to any village program and are allocated across programs according to a formula calculated using the royal accounting principles.

Appendix D – Abbingdon Grant Evaluation Report

Evaluation report on activities performed in pursuit of the objectives as written in the troll abatement grant so generously provided by Her Majesty the Queen and administered by the Duke and Duchess of Arbuckle, Wales.

Submitted on this date of 30 June, 2016

by the Right Honorable Mayor Peate Adwir Gittins

Lord Mayor

Village of Abbingdon

Isle of Thatch

Preface by Lord Mayor Gittens.

The village elders moved quickly to establish a project evaluation committee by posting a notice in the *Shire Cryer*, inviting proposals for evaluation services. All bids were read by a committee of village elders and the final evaluation contractor was selected by sealed vote of all village elders.

Wigglesworth and Tonky, Ltd. (W&T, Ltd.) was selected as the grant evaluation consultant. W&T, Ltd. owner, Mrs. Winifred Wigglesworth, served as the principal consultant. Mr. Tonky was unavailable, more precisely— he was deceased. This made Mrs. Wigglesworth all the more desirable as the company representative.

But the manner in which Mr. Tonky met his unfortunate end is more to the point. He was stewed by Glasgow trolls in 1996, whilst leading a weekend excursion of the Charred Truffle Society. Both Mr. Tonky and his pet, Skwinky, a pig, naturally, were ambushed to the horror of all present. No trace of Mr. Tonky was ever found, but Skwinky's hand-embroidered collar was discovered and returned to the grieving Mrs. Tonky providing small but tangible solace.

Mrs. Wigglesworth (Mrs. W), devoted business partner of Mr. Tonky for more than a dozen years, pledged her life's work to troll abatement after his disappearance. She therefore brought unparalleled insight, experience, and dedication to her professional work.

The village council invited Mrs. W to present her evaluation plan before the village elders, to explain the data she would collect, and to provide a schedule for her visits throughout the year. Mrs. W made an excellent presentation and, living up to her credentials, gave the village elders full faith and confidence that she would capably report the outcomes of our troll abatement grant program.

I am proud to say that despite several daunting obstacles and circumstances, the Village of Abbingdon completed the project and achieved all objectives to 100% as described herein.

In evidence of our successful project and faithful implementation of the grant proposal, I hereby submit this Final Evaluation Report authored by Mrs. W and unanimously approved by the Village Elders of the Village of Abbingdon.

Faithfully yours,

Peate Adwir Gittins

Evaluation Narrative

The project evaluation committee (which the villagers referred to as the e-comy) was formed and met for the first time on the 27th day after the decree of award was gleefully received by Lord Mayor Gittins. Mrs. Margaret Wigglesworth, the evaluation consultant under contract, and author of this report (hereafter consultant or Mrs. W, as it suits the author), was employed within a fortnight of the receipt of said decree.

The consultant met with the e-comy members, who were convened by Lord Mayor Gittins. The e-comy was comprised of seven members including three village elders, the lord mayor, the Abbingdon School headmaster, the village constable Mr. Walter Abernathy, the project superintendent, and two village members at-large: Wisty Wedlock, homemakeranxiuosly-in-waiting, and one Angus Hornbuckle, aged 13 and a half, an 8th form student from the Abbingdon Comprehensive School. Master Hornbuckle was ostensibly included to provide diversity of perspective from the village youth, but in reality he was recruited because the headmaster desired to keep Angus under his watch.

The e-comy met twice per month during the first three months and once per month for the remaining nine months. An exception occurred in September when the e-comy met five times owing to urgent circumstances, which shall be explained in due course.

The purpose of each meeting is set forth in a meeting agenda (maintained in village elder meeting records), and each agenda was prepared at the end of the previous meeting, with the exception of the first meeting agenda when there was no previous meeting upon which to rely. Hence, this first agenda was drafted by Mrs. W and reviewed and approved by Lord Mayor Gittins. The e-comy was facilitated and chaired by the lord mayor, except during September when the project superintendent filled in for his excellency, an absence which will be explained in due course.

The e-comy agenda commonly included a report by the superintendent on progress made toward achievement of grant objectives since the prior meeting, a data review as analyzed by Mrs. W, recommendations from e-comy members, and group problem-solving. After each meeting, a summary was written, copied, and distributed to all members.

Summary of the Achievement of Objectives

Objectives	Achievement
Objective 1 – Build troll habitat by reconstructing the Firth of Forth Bridge and fishing platforms within 12 months of grant approval, as measured by a completed, safe and functional structure.	100%
Objective 2 – Within the project period, provide troll safety certification training for 200 adults with 90% earning a Class A Troll Safety Certificate, as measured by rosters of participants, attendance records, and a list of adults earning national Class A Troll Safety Certification.	100%
Objective 3 – Within the project period, provide troll safety curriculum and instruction for all school children that results in 90% of all children earning a troll safety rating of A or B as measured by student attendance, lesson plans, and records of children earning national troll safety ratings of A or B.	100%
Objective 4 – Create and implement a troll safety plan for the Village of Abbingdon that results in zero children stewed or dipped during the project year, to be measured by stewing/dipping instances, installation of electronic monitoring and alert systems, agendas and sign-in sheets from planning meetings, and a published troll safety plan adopted by the village elders.	100%

Description of Grant Activities

Reconstruction of the bridge was the largest grant budget item and central to restoring a troll-safe environment on the Isle of Thatch and the Village of Abbingdon.

The Lord Mayor Gittins advertised the superintendent's post in the *Shire Cryer* upon receipt of the funding letter. By the expiration of the advert, however, no qualified applications were received. The lord mayor took it upon himself, from his own resources, to journey in search of a proper candidate who could fulfil all position requirements. Lord Mayor Gittins travelled by ferry across the Firth and hired a wagon to carry him on his journey on which he met with many, many lord mayors of the villages along his route, drank many cups of tea, and quaffed countless pints of stout.

The details of Lord Mayor Gittin's search for a superintendent are not chronicled here due to the 24-day length and strenuous nature of his journey. In addition, this activity predated the first e-comy meeting. Suffice it to say that his powers of survival, tenacity, and persuasion were tested, and the unpadded splintered wagon seat contributed in no small way to his great discomfort.

Upon the Lord Mayor Gittins' return, the entire village was relieved that the lord mayor secured in Ms. Heddy Wyn, second cousin to a descendent of Llwelyn the Great. Heddy was just the right woman for the job. The e-comy members beamed with confidence that the grant activities would proceed precisely according to schedule and without major difficulties.

The urgency of reconstructing the bridge imbued each meeting of the e-comy with a high sense of seriousness and tensions in these meetings ran high. But securing a superintendent with such a confident manner lowered the tension and eased the minds of the membership.

The path to achievement of a project's objectives is often more like the village's winding cobblestone streets than a smoothly paved London boulevard, and almost never as imagined by a planning committee or grant writer. This project, while successful, was no different in that regard. The first barrier to success presented itself during only the second week, soon after Superintendent Heddy Wyn arrived on the island with her family.

An e-comy meeting was scheduled for the day in question, a Wednesday. The members were gathered at the community hall and sat enjoying plates of baked goodies prepared by their Mrs. Walter Abernathy. On that evening, the lord mayor commented carelessly that one of Mrs. Walter Abernathy's scones was a bit dry and lacking in butter. The poor woman burst into tears, shrieked horribly and fled out into the street. Mr. Walter Abernathy, her husband, hurried after her apologizing for the disruption as he trotted red-faced out the door to comfort his wailing wife. Mrs. Abernathy's wailing echoed up and down the village, echoing off the cobbles, and in spite of the lack of an accompanying pot banging and clashing, the villagers of Abbingdon mistook the dear woman's scone distress for a troll alarm. The children were collected and herded into their homes. Across the village was heard the percussive sound of doors and windows banging shut.

The lord mayor later visited the Abernathy cottage to apologize for his insensitive comment and to assure Mrs. Walter Abernathy that he had the utmost respect for her unmatched baking prowess, and that he had no doubt that, as all the village cooks were being forced to economize, she was finding butter in short supply with the bridge out. He emphasized that soon she would be able to cross freely once again to the Mumbles where she could buy all the butter she wanted, and that her scones would once again be the marvel of the island. Mrs. Walter Abernathy thanked the lord mayor as Walter patted her gently on the shoulder. In recognition of the lord mayor's gracious attempt to make amends, she insisted he stay for tea and she fed the lord mayor and Mr. Walter Abernathy nice plates of pickled herring and sliced cucumbers.

At the August e-comy meeting, a much more serious situation developed that led to weekly e-comy meetings in the month of September. The lord mayor was always the last to arrive on Wednesday because on those after-noons he served as the Abbingdon Village football coach. He trained the children on the village pitch, blowing his whistle and organizing drills, and trying to keep Angus Hornbuckle from committing fouls and booting the ball out-of-bounds and into the thatch.

Walter Abernathy took note of the time being 6:00 p.m. sharp, and as the self-appointed sergeant at arms of the e-comy, he tapped his teacup with a spoon to collect the attention of the group. All moved to the conference table, ending their trailing conversations with the sound of scraping chairs as the clumps of people separated. They seated themselves around the grand oak table that had been hand-carved by legendary Willy the Whittler from a stupendous Welsh oak, which once washed onshore after a violent storm.

Willy was devilishly clever with wood and he carved the table as smooth and flat as the Firth in a doldrums on a summer day. He'd even carved royal crests around the edge of the thick slab, lions and griffins, swords and crowns. Willy had hoped to sell it to a royal and retire but he could never make a royal connection and his plans fell through. Willy was re-signed to use it as a worktable, but the lord mayor heard about Willy's creation and arranged to buy it for the Abbingdon Community Meeting Hall. Willy was disappointed that his masterpiece would not grace the halls at Conway Castle, but was somewhat soothed by the place of honor it would hold in his own village where he could keep it well-polished.

Walter Abernathy called the meeting to order and recorded attendance. The absences of the lord mayor and Angus Hornbuckle were noted but no alarm was registered at their tardiness.

The meeting was about to commence when Angus—with bright red cheeks, thatch-like red hair, and a moustache of perspiration—burst inside the hall and stood panting wide-eyed in his jumper, shorts, and trainers.

The adults turned their heads to look at Angus when they heard the door open, expecting to greet the lord mayor following him inside. Mr. Walter Abernathy spoke, "It's about time Angus, come and take your place. Is the lord mayor coming along just now?"

"He ain't coming to the meeting, sir. He's gone missing, sir," the boy replied.

At this news, Mrs. Walter Abernathy dropped a full platter of cucumber finger sandwiches. She appeared very likely to faint, so Mr. Abernathy moved quickly to steady her and ushered her to a chair and gently patted her hand.

The boy was given a chair and a glass of milk and asked to tell what he'd seen. This is a summary of the boy's description of events.

The lord mayor was leading football practice as he does each Wednesday. The pitch was damp with fog as is often the case each afternoon on the isle. Lord Mayor Gittins was tending goal in a drill and each player was to attempt to score a goal against him. Any player to score was excused from running laps.

Angus had his try and the ball flew high, up and over the top post, and then rolled to the edge of the pitch. Angus was a feared sweeper with a strong leg but nobody could guess where his cannon-like shots would land and most of the time the opposing team would fall to the ground and cover their faces when Angus cocked his leg for a shot.

"The lord mayor ran around behind the net to collect the ball and that was when it happened." Angus sat and stared at them chewing on a chocolate biscuit.

"What happened!," the adults all chimed at once.

"Well, you see, a troll was hiding in the thatch, there at the end of the pitch. I think it was waiting for one of us kids to chase that ball, sir. But the lord mayor ran to retrieve that ball and the troll grabbed him instead. Why that troll put the lord mayor on his shoulder as easy as if he were a bundle of thatch! Then that troll pushed back into the thatch and it and the lord mayor was gone."

"Were gone," advised the headmaster.

"Yes sir, they was gone indeed," agreed Angus.

Angus described the scene and how terrified children began to cry and scream until one of the older girls, Leslie Hardhammer, demanded that they stop their crying at once and act like proper Welsh children. She then gathered them into a line at the end of the pitch furthest from the thatch. The children were paired up to clasp hands and walk very quickly to town, which they did amid much sniffling.

"Leslie told me to come here to tell the e-comy what happened. She took the rest to their homes."

Mrs. Walter Abernathy recovered herself and declared that a village meeting must be called at once. She then left with Walter to obtain pots from her kitchen cupboards to alert the village.

Soon every man, woman, and tightly-grasped child were assembled in the village square to hear the news: their beloved lord mayor had been abducted. A search party of able-bodied men led by Mr. Walter Abernathy soon scoured the thatch fields with lanterns held high to light the darkness. At dawn the next morning, the bedraggled posse shuffled back into town discouraged, bent from exhaustion and hunger. Mrs. Walter Abernathy prepared a full breakfast at the village hall and after the men had quieted their growling stomachs, they retired to their homes for rest.

The e-comy met in the afternoon to discuss the lord mayor's abduction as a potential barrier to successful achievement of the goals of the grant whilst they also hoped he would soon be found safe or released. The members agreed that the work of the grant must go on regardless, so the e-comy voted unanimously to have the Superintendent Heddy Wyn assume the e-comy chair in the lord mayor's absence.

The superintendent's first act was to recommend that a portion of the grant funding be spent to employ a troll hunter who would locate and rescue the lord mayor. At first this suggestion was met with some reluctance. Some members argued that if funds were diverted, the goal may not be reached to rebuild the bridge, and that spending funds to save the lord mayor could put all the children at risk for generations. There was a general consensus that saving the lord mayor could not be placed in higher priority than saving the village, as awful a choice as it may be. The superintendent assured the e-comy that the budget was a bit padded here and there. She explained that this was commonly done within grant budgets to allow for unforeseen circumstances. Heddy went on to assure the e-comy that while it may seem that a more normal budget adjustment might be to pay a higher price for herring or a premium for top-quality building materials, adding a line item to employ a troll hunter would not threaten to derail the project.

An amount of £10,000 was eventually approved to employ a troll hunter, and the superintendent assured the members that she'd do her best to secure a contract for less than the e-comy allotment.

A tender was soon posted around the shire, soliciting the services of an expert troll hunter. As soon as the news about the kidnapped lord mayor of Abbingdon was broadcast, bids from troll hunters poured into the island by post.

Bridge Construction

Bridge bids were solicited in July and many proposals arrived at the Tangles' Net Repair Shop. Sir Edward delivered the bids to the superintendent who chose two qualified bidders who made presentations to the e-comy members at the August meeting. Reference checks were conducted by Heddy. The e-comy was gratified to receive a goodly number of bids for the bridge, some even being received from highly-respectable Welsh firms. One bid was discarded out of hand as being incomplete, one was submitted by a fence builder who fancied expanding his operations to bridge construction, and another was from a dentist in the town of Bwlch Ifori (Ivory Gap) who had a bit of a "tippling" problem (brandy it was rumored). She misconstrued the entire tender as if it proposed extensive repairs to the lord mayor's teeth (which were famous within the shire for their luminosity).

The two firms chosen for consideration both met budgetary limitations and tender guidelines for demonstrated competence. The e-comy had ample opportunity to question the representatives as presentations were made by representatives of each firm.

In the end, the firm of Hiram Miles & Daughters was offered the contract. HM & Ds is a venerable firm that served as the general contractor for both the London Bridge (taking great umbrage to the children's tune) and the bridge over the River Kwai. Mr. Miles' reputation for quality construction was celebrated throughout the kingdom. He was even rumored to be on the Queen's shortlist for knighthood.

The elders voted unanimously to approve Mr. Miles' contract, which was signed on the spot by the lord mayor with great flourish. Daphne Miles promptly presented the elders with her first materials invoice and a plan for sourcing all necessaries immediately. That Ms. Miles was well-prepared to move forward with construction cemented the confidence of the e-comy and elders.

The following week, Mr. Miles and his younger daughter Victoria established an office and took up residence above the ale/jelly establishment of G.R. Marmalade and necessary equipment was ferried across the Firth by barge. Elder daughter Daphne established her offices on the shire side of the Firth to manage construction on that end of the bridge. This took most of the week to accomplish.

Demonstrating his ability to quickly source materials necessary for the project, Mr. Miles and daughters arranged for the needed stone to be ferried by barge to the isle. Barge after barge of the finest Cornwall limestone was delivered and stacked neatly by workmen adjacent to the new bridge footing site.

All of this work was going quite according to plan when the bargemen's union went on strike. This development produced extreme consternation with the potential for indeterminant delays in the delivery of necessary construction materials.

Superintendent Heddy Wyn convened the e-comy to discuss the impact of the strike. The moral conscience of the village, Pastor Sternly, was asked to write a plea to the queen herself through the arch bishop of Raglan to intervene in the strike and make haste to resolve it.

The villagers were relieved as all due influence was exerted on union leadership to settle their differences by the royal family, including the Duke and Duchess of Arbuckle. Within days a new contract was signed with the barge owners and delivery of materials promptly resumed.

Troll Hunter

The fate of the lord mayor put the entire village on edge. The e-comy members were under constant pressure in the village to employ a troll hunter and recover the lord mayor or, heaven forbid, his stewed-and-chewed bones.

Now lest the Duke and Duchess think to protest, owing to the protected status of trolls, these troll hunters were not employed to capture trolls or cause them harm, merely to locate and recover the lord mayor, articulated or not.

Immediately after the deadline for bid submittal, the e-comy met to consider all troll hunter applications. They narrowed the field to three potential characters with recent experience in tracking Cotswolds trolls.

Three proposals were selected and interviews arranged so all three candidates crossed the Firth together on a Friday afternoon in early September. The presence of three troll hunters in the village caused a great stir.

Their first stop, and it was of no surprise to anyone who'd been told tales as children about troll hunters, was in the ale/jelly house to quaff tankards of ale and consume loads of English muffins with jam.

Please understand that troll hunters are not your typical job applicants. Most candidates for employment wear their Sunday best to an interview and would never think to arrive late with ale on their breath, or marmalade jam stuck in their beards.

But troll hunters are not typical job applicants. Troll hunters live in the crags, peaks, and cold, damp blackened caves of the kingdom, where blind, pale creatures crawl and slither. These are places where manners are lost and forgotten because troll hunters are more concerned with being stewed than with presenting themselves with proper manners, because stewing can certainly happen to a hunter quicker than they can quaff a pint of bitter.

The three troll hunters were large, hulking men with broad shoulders bowed from years of carrying heavy packs in low caves. Adding to their fearsome appearance, they wore heavy black clothes made of rough cotton, fur and leather, hard-sole boots with steel cleats that clacked and sparked on the cobblestones as they walked shoulder to shoulder through the village; each regarded the villagers with glowering black eyes. What most distinguished each from the other was a distinctive hat. The troll hunter named Edgar wore a black bowler, Henri (for he was said to be French) wore a stained, tan-colored Paris beau which made him appear taller than the others, and the man called Ox wore a black porkpie.

At 4:30, an hour late for the first interview, the men marched forth to the village community meeting hall and were watched with both fear and interest by the villagers. They could not help but admire the courage of a man who'd hunt trolls, but they also wondered what else a man who lived so close to trolls might be capable of doing.

The three sat side-by-side on a creaking walnut wood bench outside the community hall belching loudly, making an attempt to freshen up by pulling crumbs and jam from their beards and licking their fingers. Each in turn was invited inside for an interview. After Henri was interviewed, he nodded to the others and ambled alone back to the alehouse to await the e-comy's decision. By and by he was followed by Edgar and Ox.

The Constable Walter Abernathy urged the e-comy to decide quickly. He wanted the men to return to the mainland before they had time to drink all the village ale. He was also concerned that perhaps their decision would not be well-received by the two not chosen. He did not want an incident as he didn't fancy trying to get between them.

Superintendent Heddy Wyn walked to the alehouse after the e-comy voted to select the troll hunter called Ox. She delivered the news in person and thanked all three for coming to the isle. Heddy insisted on paying their ale and jam tabs and ferry costs, which seemed to appease any ill feeling among the runners-up. She still had time to meet with Ox before the mainlander who'd brought the hunters across the Firth in his lorry (for this was during the time of the barge strike) left the island at dusk.

Ox was a descendant of the Viking invaders of old. He was a huge bear-like man with a barrel chest, broad facial features, and red cheeks. Heddy suspected his crimson cheeks were a result of the ale she watched him consume at a phenomenal rate.

Ox wiped his dripping beard with his sleeve and outlined his plan to find the mayor. He insisted that the plan must include two village volunteers. The superintendent said she'd assign two from the roster of villagers who signed on for the assembled, but yet-to-be-trained troll watch. Heddy figured that it would prove to be good training for the volunteers in understanding the habits of trolls.

Ox insisted on providing training as he was not confident of including untrained villagers in his hunt. Superintendent Heddy Wyn agreed to allow Ox to review the group and select the two volunteers he felt were up to the task of troll hunting. Ox explained that watching for trolls was much less dangerous than hunting them and that he could not be held responsible for anyone coming to harm. It made sense for Ox to train the troll watch, he was an expert. This also saved costs to the project budget for training. Heddy assured Ox that the men were volunteers and not conscripted. Ox agreed to terms and announced he'd return in two days with his equipment to organize the hunt for Lord Mayor Gittins.

Bridge Construction

A day after Ox was employed, the barge operator's strike was resolved. Soon the Firth was busy with barges of quarried stone as the contractor resumed deliveries to the Isle of Thatch. Out in the Firth between the mainland and the isle, barges began dumping stone to establish footings to support the span and serve as the foundations of cantilevers to each anchorage.

The superintendent reported to the e-comy using a chart to illustrate construction progress.

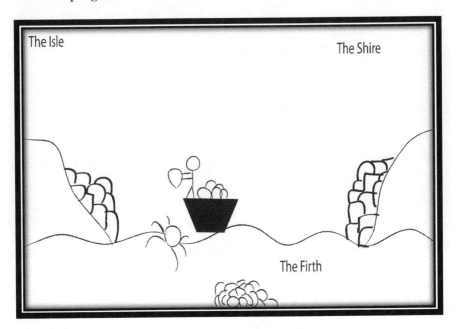

The superintendent reported positive progress month after month. Construction on the anchorage began on the isle side of the Firth while wagonloads of stone were delivered to the Shire shore and stored there.

Occasionally protests to the bridge construction were staged by Mr. Oliver McGillicudy of the shire. Mr. McGillicudy held the opinion that the bridge posed an environmental hazard to the Firth. Oliver found no support for his protests and his letters to the queen went unanswered. Rumor had it that the real purpose of the protest was that Mr. McGillicudy had a long-standing grudge against Sir Edward Tangles, who had married his childhood sweetheart, now Lady Edward Tangles, and that he was also particularly jealous of Sir Edward's knighthood. Others believed that he rather enjoyed the difficulty his relatives on the island presently had in getting across the firth to visit him. All speculation notwithstanding, the superintendent assured the e-comy that Mr. McGillicudy's singular protests would not be allowed to interfere with the construction schedule.

Troll Hunter

Ox the troll hunter returned to the isle on schedule and booked a room above the ale/jelly house. The superintendent met with Ox over a pint the afternoon of his arrival to review the preparations made since he'd been gone. Heddy scheduled a full day of troll training for the brave volunteers of the troll watch to be held out on the football pitch the following day.

Ox and the superintendent plotted out a series of seven training sessions, one on the first day and two on each of the following three days. All of the volunteers had already cleared their personal schedules to attend.

Ox presented a detailed plan to seek and recover the lord mayor, but he leveled expectations by stressing the danger of the plan. He expressed no hope that even the two volunteers he chose would not end up being "stewed and chewed," as Ox liked to call a troll hunt gone wrong.

The plan included the following steps:

1. Troll Location
2. Troll Baiting
3. Troll Diversion
4. The Raid
5. Rescue or Bone Collection

Ox explained that the first and most vital thing to be done was to locate the troll encampment. This was dangerous; he and the men would have to hike openly in the thatch fields searching on a grid and marking off townships as they were scoured for any sign of the lord mayor. It was a systematic plan to identify and map all troll huts.

Ox explained that trolls have an excellent sense of smell but, in spite of their large ears, their sense of hearing is poor. This would be to the advantage of Ox and the search team; not only because walking in thatch is a noisy business, but also because trolls grunt loudly at each other, owing to their poor hearing, and so it is often possible to hear the grunts long before the trolls are able to hear a hunter's approach.

Of course, trolls must be approached from downwind whenever possible. Since wind direction on the isle changes frequently, it is not always possible to approach trolls in a favorable wind, so Ox concocted an eye-watering, rather startling, brew of aromatic substances to mask human scent. The troll hunters were to sprinkle this concoction on themselves before setting out each day. The liquid reeked of rotted herring and the musk of an unwashed dish rag. The scent was pleasant to only trolls, who ate only fresh herring and never washed their fingers or clothing.

Training went as planned and Ox chose the two volunteers who'd performed best of the lot. The day after training finished, Ox and the two volunteers set forth with their map and compass to discover and mark all troll encampments. Each day the trio returned to the alehouse and washed off Ox's "eau de troll" as the villagers called his smelly masking cologne out back in a cistern filled with fresh water and pumice soap. After washing they would meet over pints with the e-comy to report progress. On the first two afternoons the men had nothing to report but empty thatch huts and troll stench.

On the third day the group returned to the alehouse with good news, which rapidly spread throughout the village from house-to-house. The lord mayor had been sighted and he was alive and unharmed! They observed his honor on the south side of the isle in a troll camp, sitting between two trolls, looking thin and dirty, but thankfully, as yet, un-stewed.

As the trio of hunters met the superintendent and the e-comy in the alehouse, pints of bitter were brought to them and a crowd of villagers gathered to hear about the plan to rescue the lord mayor.

Ox unrolled a parchment outlining the plan he devised on the large wooden alehouse table. On it he'd drawn a map of the isle, marking the location of the troll camp where the lord mayor was captive. He explained each detail, and all leaned their heads in close and conspiratorial as if hearing a secret. The troll camp was pitched on a small knoll. Such a location was easily defensible, and thus made a successful recovery of the lord mayor a challenge. But Ox expressed confidence that his plan would succeed.

The first step was to move delivery of fresh herring from the archway to a location south of the troll camp. This would mean that the trolls had to walk a longer distance to feed. Ox needed extra time to execute his plan, as trolls were known to gobble their food quickly.

Ox and the men had observed the camp at feeding time that day. Ox explained that when the trolls left to feed, two trolls stayed behind to guard the lord mayor. These two paced angrily about, impatient for the others to return with their portion. The two argued and wrestled with each other, hungry and unhappy about being left behind.

Ox's plan was elaborate and included catapulting a basket of herring into the encampment to distract the hungry trolls. The three men would then enter the camp from three directions at once on stilts, disguised as Lithuanian trolls with flaming red wigs and appearing exceptionally tall (but still shorter than Glasgow giant trolls, naturally).

Ox explained that Cotswolds trolls do not fear Lithuanian trolls confronted one-to-one; outnumbered three-to-two, however, and in flanking attack formation, Ox believed that their sudden appearance would strike fear in the trolls. He hoped that they'd quickly fill their pockets with catapulted herring and flee into the thatch after their mates. Herring and unwashed troll would be all the returning trolls would smell, giving Ox and the men enough time to cut loose the lord mayor and disappear into the thatch.

Ox's plan was accepted with confidence by the e-comy. The two chosen volunteers were sturdy villagers and stood forth at attention with feigned confidence and nausea concealed. The volunteers did not want to show any fear that might dampen any hope the plan conferred on the group. The villagers believed the lord mayor would be rescued, the bridge would be soon completed, and the village would once again be safe from the troll menace.

The mood of the e-comy was joyful as its members departed the alehouse. The fishing contractor was instructed to immediately begin depositing her load of herring on the south side of the island. On the first afternoon, one or two of the slower trolls moped about the arch licking the trough edges at feeding time. But soon the wind caught their noses, and as they scented the breeze blowing northward across the thatch, they dashed wildly southward, noses to the wind. Step one of the plan was now in place and working just as Ox predicted.

On the morning of the rescue attempt, fog clung thick and wet to the edges of the thatch, like the marmalade in Ox's beard. Most of the villagers had a difficult night's sleep, and many lamps were lit early along the cobbled lanes. A large group of well-wishers gathered at the alehouse to see off Ox and the volunteers. Pastor Sternly gave a benediction to ask for favor and good fortune in their rescue attempt. The prayer left Mrs. Walter Abernathy as dewy as the morning.

The Rescue

The details of the rescue attempt were related to this evaluator in an interview with Ox the troll hunter on the day after its conclusion. The villagers were relieved to have the lord mayor out of the thatch fields, where he had caused agricultural disaster. The farmers feared that his mere unlucky presence in the fields might result in another crop crisis. Thatch farmers are a superstitious lot.

This is a record Ox's version of events transcribed faithfully as he retold them to this evaluator.

"Me and me volunteers waded into the thatch an hour before feeding time, following the landmarks we noted on the map previous, at what time we discovered the lord mayor's whereabouts. We arrived at the camp downwind and hid ourselves in the thatch. By and by there came a strong stink of herring blown in off the Firth, which was an improvement to the stench o' them trolls.

Before we smelled them fish, trolls began raising their great bumpy noses to the wind and grunting and garbling to each other. Them trolls has a powerful sense of smell, as you may well know.

Soon enough them trolls began to lumber off down the trail going south. I whispered to the volunteers it was time fer them ta circle away in opposite directions and get into position. They was told ta wait fer me signal—a blast wit me Lithuanian troll's horn.

I was worried when tree of dem trolls was stayed behind ta watch the lord mayor. His lordship was tied by one foot to dat tree wit a woven thatch rope. I chucked some scones up onto the heads of them trolls and each one thought da other one done the deed and they started ta shove each other about. The lord mayor was watchin' them brutes and he hid his self behind the tree so as not to be trampled in da scuffle.

Them trolls commenced to wrestling and then two had da third one pinned on the ground and was a sittin' a top o' him. Dat one what was overcome grunted in a high whine and those other two climbed offa him and they laughed at him lyin' there. Then those two walked off down the trail right quick, noses high upwind toward them herring.

Dat troll what the others had pinned rolled up onto his side and he threw a wicked look at da lord mayor as if he was da cause of him gettin' left back. Why then dat troll he grabbed up a handful of dust and pebbles and threw it hard at the tree where da lord mayor hid behind. The rocks clattered off the tree and the dust blew up in a cloud.

Dat was when I blew me ram's horn and da three of us put on our horned hats and wigs, we and climbed up our stilts and walked out into the clearing."

"But what about the catapult and the basket of herring?" I asked Ox.

"Oh, dat got scrapped as a catapult is mighty heavy and noisy to push through thatch and we didn't want ta be carryin' a bushel of herring neither in case the wind were ta shift on us."

"I see, please continue."

"We took dat bag o' Wisty Wedlock's lemon scones and we was hurling them scones at dat troll (more about Wisty's scones later). Dat brute saw me first and he jumped up snarling like a mad bear to attack me. He grunted loud and he crouched low to da dirt like he was fixin' to pick potatoes and then he started ta charge at me. Dem volunteers come out of da thatch and whacked him proper wit a scone apiece and we had dat troll hemmed in tight. Dat troll stood up and he turned round and round. Now trolls is strong and trolls is ugly, but trolls isn't brave and only just smart enough ta count three. So just as soon as dat troll saw he was outnumbered by Lithuanian trolls, his confidence drained right out o' him. He turned and ran off down dat trail. We all three of us dismounted our stilts straight away and took off dem wigs and da lord mayor looked terrified that he was trading one sort of troll problem for 'nother. I sliced away da rope from his leg and he was overjoyed to see that we wasn't actually Lithuanian trolls and den we all made our way quick as a wink back to da village."

Lord Mayor's Return

As the rescue team led by Ox returned with the lord mayor, the village erupted into spontaneous celebration. Villagers poured out of their homes and carried out tables and covered them with white and green checkered tablecloths and platters and baskets of food. The alehouse rolled out three kegs of bitter to sweeten the celebration. Mrs. Walter Abernathy set to baking and laid out a baked goods and pickled herring feast, and not a soul went home hungry.

Ox and his two assistants were hailed as heroes and, after a bath, the lord mayor was embraced and welcomed home. Reginald Marmalade even played the bag pipes while Wisty Wedlock did a jig that was well appreciated by the crowd. Several of the church elders and Pastor Sternly formed a human barricade around the Maypole in case Wisty became overly enthusiastic under the spell of celebration and ale.

Back to Work

The lord mayor was encouraged by the village elders to take a holiday and recover his strength after his ordeal. But the lord mayor thanked them and declined. He insisted that a good night's sleep would be sufficient, and he'd recover best by resuming his duties. The lord mayor knew now better than anyone, except perhaps Ox, the danger trolls posed for his village.

Lord mayor called an e-comy meeting the very next morning after his rescue to receive a status update on the progress being made toward achievement of the grant objectives. He was pleased that in his absence Heddy and the elders had pushed the work forward.

By the end of January, the project was on track to meet all benchmarks set forth in the grant. The pie graph below illustrates the summary of progress to that point.

Grant Progress

The pie graph below shows achievement of each objective by percentage through January.

Achievement of Objectives September - January

50%

100%

63%

55%

- Objective 1 - Bridge
- Objective 2 - Adult Ed
- Objective 3 - Child Ed
- Objective 4 - Troll Safety Plan

Troll watch training was scheduled and prioritized. Ox agreed to stay on a few more days to assist with training, and the volunteers who'd played an important role in the search and rescue accepted paid positions as lieutenants in the troll watch command. The seriousness of the troll situation conferred a need for discipline in the ranks. The men and women were proud to serve their village and they rotated on shifts around the clock to ensure villager safety.

Bridge

By mid-year, bridge construction was ahead of schedule and all footings were completed. The superintendent was confident that she could complete the plan in time for the villagers to walk across to the July "Tawe Fest" celebration in the Mumbles.

The lord mayor's return relieved the added stress of e-comy leadership that the superintendent had assumed during the lord mayor's absence. The e-comy discussed a proposal to return troll feeding to the trough beneath the arch outside of town. This decision was met with some resistance by the villagers who liked the distant feeding established to support the lord mayor's rescue. Several villagers spoke up against feeding at the archway because it had become a curiosity for the children. Villagers feared that one of the children would soon be abducted.

What convinced the elders in the end was a request from the fisherfolk who submitted a claim for additional fuel and labor to motor all the way around the island. This extra cost was added to worries that the weather would soon turn foul, and that landing on the south shore would become too hazardous. The superintendent also argued that feeding the trolls under the arch made better sense because it was closer to the new bridge, thereby facilitating transition of the trolls to their new habitat. The arch also provided good training for the trolls, as they would be living under arches soon enough.

Bridge construction continued, according to plan and ahead of schedule. Superintendent Heddy Wyn was an able construction manager and saw to it that all materials selected were of high quality, and that below market prices were negotiated. She supervised the project with firmness and diplomacy, and Hiram Miles and daughters lived up to their reputation as master stonemasons and bridge builders.

The troll watch kept up regular shifts. Only two troll intrusions were recorded that resulted in full alarms during the first nine months of operation, and the electronic troll warning system worked as expected. None in the village was happier about its installation than Mrs. Walter Abernathy.

Troll Safety Education

Adult Troll Safety classes were conducted according to the schedule outlined in the grant proposal. All adults in the village except one passed the training. The percentage of adults that passed the troll test and earned a Class A Troll Safety Certification are shown in the graph below.

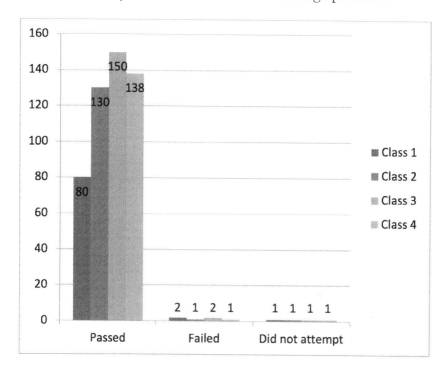

The shire council provided a teacher for the adult classes as promised. He was an experienced troll safety instructor from Bath, and he came to stay on the isle for two-week stays throughout the year whilst classes were in session.

It should be noted that the number of adults who took the courses (504) is higher than the number of adults who live in the village. This is because two of the villagers took the course each time it was offered. One adult, Odmer Pattywhack, had to retake the course four times due to his failure to pass the Class A Troll Safety Certificate test. Whilst it is not a requirement that all citizens hold the class A, Odmer did not want to be the only person in Abbingdon without a certificate, as this was considered a sign of good citizenship. Besides, Odmer aspired to join the troll watch, and the class A certificate was a requirement for membership. After Odmer failed the test for a fourth time, Master Turnbuckle, the teacher, petitioned the Department of Troll Safety for an honorary class A certificate and personally vouched for Odmer's competency in all aspects of troll safety. The certificate was granted and Mrs. Walter Abernathy baked Odmer a cake to celebrate his graduation.

Wisty Wedlock, a lonely spinster, also repeated the class, but not because she failed the certification exam. She simply enjoyed the subject and for a time fancied the shire instructor Master Turnbuckle Cadwerner. Wisty fancied "Cady," as she called him, as he bore a striking resemblance to the lord mayor, with whom she was hopelessly in love. Wisty attended the first two courses but had no luck in catching the master's eye. Wisty began to lose interest in Master Turnbuckle after Ox the troll hunter led the rescue of the lord mayor.

Bridge Completion

The e-comy meeting in May was charged with excitement. Every villager during the past month had walked to the Firth to observe that their new bridge was nearing completion. The security gates at both ends of the bridge were erected before decking was applied. This ensured that none of the trolls crossed over to the shire whilst the bridge lay unsecured. The rails were designed to curve outward gently, like rolling waves, as if the bridge had been dropped gently into the Firth the rails splashing outward along its edges. This design gave the bridge an artistic elegance, and it prevented trolls from climbing up and over from beneath. Security gates at both ends of the span provided ample safety to prevent troll migration off the isle. The deck was completed and the rail was installed across half the span. Meanwhile, underneath the bridge, fishing platforms were loaded on a barge and floated in place and secured to the pillars.

Everyone's mood in the village was upbeat because, of course, completing the bridge meant that soon the trolls would move underneath it, and the villagers would finally be safe.

At the e-comy meeting in May, the superintendent announced that the bridge would be ready to host the trolls one week hence. The members cheered, and laughed, and slapped each other on their backs. Mrs. Walter Abernathy was commissioned to bake a large cake for the ribbon cutting ceremony.

The superintendent presented her plan to the e-comy to entice the trolls to inhabit the bridge. The plan was needed because even though a bridge is a troll's favorite habitat, with the trolls' poor eyesight and because their huts were built deep in the thatch, it was doubtful that the trolls were aware of the new bridge under construction. It might take decades for the trolls to relocate if they were left to find it on their own, so Heddy devised a plan to help speed things up.

The plan included a construction of a temporary wooden plank with rope rails from the isle to the arches where the fishing platforms would be piled high with herring. Over the next week the trough would be dragged a distance each day from the arch toward the bridge, bringing the trolls closer and closer to their new home. Sir Edward Tangles would employ his horse and cart to drag the trough along, and the fisherfolk would fill the trough at each new location. The villagers were warned to be extra vigilant, as the trolls may feel somewhat disoriented by moving the trough and wander into town. Troll watch was put on high alert and extra patrols were scheduled throughout the week.

The e-comy approved the superintendent's plan and spirits were high as the meeting adjourned. Members talked with excitement about the Mumbles and the coming Tawe Fest, and the shopping they'd soon be able to do whenever they wanted just by walking across the bridge.

On the first day that the trough was moved there were six troll alerts in the village. The wind shifted and the scent of herring blew north over the Firth, so the trolls couldn't find the trough. They wandered about sullen, hungry, and looking for food. The e-comy called an emergency meeting to discuss the matter. Superintendent Heddy Wyn explained that when the wind blew in from the south side of the island it carried the scent of herring away from the thatch and toward the bridge. Because of the wind direction and troll's poor eyesight, the trolls couldn't find the scent or the trough.

The superintendent proposed to grind up a portion of herring and lay down an oily trail from the arch to the new trough location. The plan was well-received and Heddy was given the go-ahead.

The following afternoon, a portion of the herring was delivered to the butcher shop for grinding. A large, slopping bucket of ground herring was prepared and the troll watch hauled the mixture to the site, pouring it out along the skid trail left from dragging the trough to its new location.

Problems with the plan arose as soon as the trolls arrived. Trolls have small brains and are quick to anger; additionally, the trolls were hungry because they had not eaten the day before. To say that the trolls were out of sorts is to put it mildly. Finding the ground herring must have appeared to the trolls as though hors d'oeuvres were being served. Hence the trolls—being ravenously hungry—began to push and pull each other like ill-behaved children at an Easter egg hunt picking up the bits of herring and shoving them hungrily into their mouths, fingers and all.

Soon the jostling turned to trading blows and before long there was a tangle of trolls rolling on the ground in a cloud of dust, with arms and legs waving and thrashing about. Needless to say, the trolls did not follow the trail of the fish to the trough, for they grew tired, and the kerfuffle had disturbed the oily trail. Now the trolls were dirtier and hungrier than when they had arrived, and their mood was, if such a thing were possible for a troll, even more foul than when they'd arrived. Off they tramped grumbling, garbling and grunting loudly amongst themselves, tossing elbows at any that dared to crowd their way along.

The troll watch commander reported the events to the superintendent, who called together the e-comy to share news of the failure and to brainstorm a new strategy. The e-comy mood was gloomy, and a sense of desperation was evoked by Heddy Wyn who paced nervously, anxious to finish the job she'd started, and finish it well.

The lord mayor remained steadfast and calm in the face of this trouble. He suggested that a short-term contract be offered to Ox the troll hunter to advise and assist them. The e-comy jumped at the suggestion and Mutton Cornwall was sent out as a courier with a wax-sealed proposal to find Ox. Word spread throughout the village that Ox might soon be returning.

Tongues were wagging all around the village as every man, woman, and child rehashed the situation and witnesses recounted the sight of angry trolls thrashing about in the dust after scraps of herring. Everyone had an opinion about the proper way to relocate the trolls. Ideas discussed ran the gambit from setting the thatch alight to drive them out, to setting out pots of ale for them to drink until the trolls passed out like so many university students along the Mumbles, then pile them on carts and trundle them to the bridge and deposit the trolls nearby. But all those plans were just so much hot air as nobody seriously wanted to waste good ale on trolls, and not a cart in the village could carry even the smallest of the trolls without permanent axle damage.

It was at this time that villagers noted the absence of Wisty Wedlock. Her absence was noted particularly because of her famous affection for Ox. During the troll hunter's stay on the isle months earlier, Wisty had taken to baking lemon scones for Ox. Wisty's baking prowess did not improve her prospects with men on the isle. Wisty's scones were so well known for their weight and density that Hiram Miles briefly considered using them for anchoring material during the barge union strike. Ox, unfortunately, before he could be warned off, lost a front tooth biting into one. But he took this setback with his characteristic pragmatism, commenting that the trolls would fear him all the more with a gap-tooth snarl. He assured Wisty that her scones were good slingshot projectiles and that with sufficient slow-cooking would make delicious dumplings in his 10-day mutton stew. Wisty melted. Each day she baked Ox more scones throughout his time on the isle.

Wisty wasn't to be found in the village so the troll watch organized a search party. The searchers soon found Wisty—to the amazement of the troll watch—at the arch, with a bucket of herring, hand feeding two young trolls. This was dangerous and clearly in violation of article 5, subsection 2.3 of the Edinburgh Protocol of the Royal Society for Troll Abatement. Such an act placed her in the greatest physical jeopardy, not to mention it placed her Class A Troll Safety Certificate in jeopardy of permanent revocation.

Wisty was ordered to leave the arch, abandon the bucket, and return to the village at once. She protested, but soon complied and was escorted to sit before the e-comy in a hastily-called meeting where she was to answer for her reckless behavior.

While the search for Wisty was conducted, the courier, Mutton Cornwall, crossed the Firth and located Ox at an alehouse called the Trolls' Lair along the Gower. Ox sat alone at a table devouring a large basin of 10-day mutton stew with lemon dumplings, pulling carrots from his wiry beard and dropping them back into the stew. Mutton explained about the troll relocation troubles and delivered the sealed proposal from the e-comy which Ox tore open and read thoughtfully. Ox agreed to come at once and returned with Mutton on the barge.

Meanwhile, Wisty explained herself to the e-comy. Her foggy eyes dripped and tears rolled over her plump and rosy cheeks in rivulets. She explained that she'd had taken to hand feeding the two juvenile trolls early on during bridge construction. She'd never had children of her own—being the only spinster in the village. She feared she had no prospect of improving her situation and it seemed natural to take a kind and motherly hand to the hungry young trolls. Mrs. Walter Abernathy wept with Wisty and moved beside her to give comfort and offer her pickles, cookies, and a needle point-adorned hankie.

The lord mayor maintained a stiff upper lip and reprimanded Wisty, he did so firmly but more gently than he thought she deserved, not wishing to send her into another paroxysm of weeping. He reminded her that she was a valued community member who must not endanger herself or others with dangerous troll feeding, no matter how empathetic the e-comy might be towards her dreams of wedded bliss. Wisty agreed to stop feeding the trolls. As punishment, her Class A Troll Safety Certificate was put on a three-month probationary status and she was ordered to immediately enroll in a remedial troll safety course.

While Wisty explained herself, Ox entered the hall. Mutton Cornwall followed behind, quite red-faced and breathless at having to keep up with the long-striding Ox.

Ox asked why Wisty sat under the judgement of the e-comy and the superintendent explained what she'd done. Ox made no comment, just parted his lips slightly displaying the large black gap in his dentition—almost a smile, but nobody could be quite certain, because Ox was never known to smile.

After Wisty was thoroughly reprimanded and the matter put to rest, the difficulty in moving the trolls to the bridge was explained to Ox. He questioned them about the steps already taken and he nodded and grunted.

Several members would later swear that several times Ox had winked at Wisty, although others would claim that Ox often appeared to blink erratically due to his wild and bushy eyebrows.

Ox deliberated, pulled at his beard and the e-comy members stared hopefully at him, shifting uneasily in their chairs. I can't say what they were thinking, but for myself, I was desperately anxious that Ox would have a solution.

Ox sat forward suddenly and banged his fist on the table, saying only, "Got 'er" causing all e-comy members to snap back in their seats and sending an avalanche of scones off the platter in the center of the great oak table. Ox then set forth a plan, which to the astonishment of all, depended on Wisty. Ox explained that he would be able to move the trolls in one afternoon to their new bridge, and all he needed was a horse-drawn cart and one basket of herring. The rest of the daily herring delivery was to be poured out along the fishing platforms now installed under the bridge.

The plan was simple: Wisty had been feeding the young trolls, so Ox asserted that she was—without realizing it—a troll charmer. The e-comy sat back in their chairs and stared open-mouthed at Wisty. Ox told the e-comy that her talent was indeed a rare gift, and that in all his days hunting trolls, he'd only met one other troll charmer, Helga Klinkowikz. Helga was the great, granddaughter of Omar Klinkowikz—who was rumored to be half troll, which made Helga 1/16th troll, at least.

The lord mayor wanted to know how Ox could be certain since Wisty had only fed young trolls and they surely were less fearful of people and not as dangerous as fully-grown trolls. But Ox explained the nature of trolls and how protective they are of their young. Were Wisty not a troll charmer, she surely would have been abducted by the trolls, stewed and chewed, as it were.

Ox maintained that Wisty was indeed a troll charmer and she held the key to moving the trolls. Wisty would be sent out to feed the young trolls the next afternoon as they found her that very day. But rather than sitting under the arch, Wisty would sit on the back of the cart, driven by Ox, with the basket of herring. He'd drive that cart along slowly toward the bridge. The adult trolls—who Ox said were without doubt keeping watch from the thatch as Wisty fed their young ones—would have no choice but to follow along as the cart moved toward the bridge.

Ox maintained that as soon as the trolls got within 500 meters of the bridge, they'd be able to see the bridge and, with luck, pick up the scent of herring under the arches. They'd snatch up their young'uns as they passed by the cart. This moment, Ox explained, would be the truest test of Wisty's troll charmer powers. If Wisty were indeed a troll charmer, each of the trolls would wink at her when passing the cart.

(Mrs. W ponders the meaning of Ox's winks at Wisty throughout the e-comy meeting...)

The e-comy agreed to the plan and adjourned the meeting to take part in preparations. The lord mayor went with the superintendent to speak with the fishing contractor and to view the gangway on which the trolls would walk to make their way onto the fishing platforms beneath the bridge arches.

Mr. Walter Abernathy convened a meeting of the troll watch. The members were to flank the trolls along the path to the bridge to ensure none strayed and got lost along the way.

Preparations in the village were a bustle of activity. The villagers gathered in groups all about town discussing the plan and debating its prospects for success and the stunning news that Wisty might be a troll charmer. Sir Edward Tangles worked at his shop to weave and knot together two nets which the troll watch were to carry for the purpose of capturing any rogue trolls who resisted moving to the bridge, although this was not part of Ox's plan. Ox considered it a waste of time and resources as no net made by humans could secure a full grown Cotswolds troll. Mutton Cornwall fed his horse special oats and applied mink oil to its harness.

The following morning the entire village met in the square. Sir Tangles brought the nets and Ox rode with Wisty on the horse cart, carrying a basket of herring in the rear.

With all preparations made and everyone present, the plan was put into action. The troll watch was dispatched first on their routes to take up flanking positions along the route to the bridge.

Ox shook the shining reins and the horse lurched forward bumping over the cobbles and pulled the wagon out of the village toward the arch. When the wagon was in place beside the arch, Wisty called out, and soon two young trolls pushed out of the thatch and trotted up behind the wagon where Wisty sat beside the basket of fish. After each troll was handed a herring, Ox clicked his tongue and the horse pulled the cart slowly forward. As it did, the young trolls ambled along behind and Ox watched as the thatch quivering and rustling along the edge of the pitch.

The juvenile trolls followed the cart greedily sucking down herring they took from Wisty's hand. As the cart led the young trolls away from the thatch, adult trolls parted the reeds and poked out their heads to look, grunting and snorting worriedly among themselves.

Soon the adults pushed out into view to follow their young ones as the wagon rolled on slowly toward the distant bridge followed by the chewing, slurping young trolls. Wisty spoke to them quietly and the adult trolls plodded along at a distance behind.

After a time, the trolls looked beyond the wagon at the bridge garbling with excitement, a serendipitous breeze blew into their faces from the Firth, on it they scented the herring under the arches. Just as Ox had predicted, those trolls snatched up their young and rushed past the wagon to run to the bridge, up the gangway, and to the fishing platforms. Ox reported that as they passed the wagon, each of them winked at Wisty, putting to rest any doubt that she was indeed a troll charmer after all.

The troll watch members were the first to return to the village with the news of success, and the villagers prepared the square for the triumphant return of Ox and Wisty. The villagers celebrated all day and late into the night. The lord mayor gave a long speech to the crowd. He recognized the superintendent and Ox with specially engraved ale mugs and he lauded the hard work of the troll watch. Of course he thanked Mrs. Walter Abernathy who had worked so diligently all year to feed the e-comy. His lordship encouraged Mrs. Abernathy to put her pot and spoon back into her kitchen and spend restful afternoons on her front porch.

The celebration ended with a parade to the bridge and the whole village walked together singing songs with arms around each other. The celebrating crowd walked across the bridge to the Mumbles, where they drank bitters, stouts, porters, reds and barley wine, and they sang victory songs and gave speeches to praise the courage of Ox and Wisty and the skill of Ms. Heddy Wyn, the project superintendent, and sang "God Save the Queen" in honor of Her Majesty's generous grant that saved the village, rebuilt the bridge, and restored the thatch industry.

In Summary

Abbingdon's troll abatement grant was a resounding success, all barriers were overcome and all objectives were fully achieved. Not one child was stewed (or even dipped) during the project year, the bridge was completed on time and within budget, and 100% of the trolls were relocated to new habitat on the arches beneath the bridge.

All the villagers now hold Class A Troll Safety Certificates, or an honorary certificate. And, the villagers discovered they had a resident troll charmer who is now married to the country's foremost troll hunter. Yes, Ox moved to the Isle of Thatch permanently, where he and Wisty were married in a beautiful, flower-festooned ceremony under the stone arch in the new Wisty Meadows Memorial Park on what was said to be the most perfect day of the year.

Mrs. W can report that even the trolls cried.

The End

Appendix E – Beat Sheet Concept

Grant Sections Beats

Musicians play music on a time signature based on a number of beats per measure. Standard time is 4:4 or four beats per measure, known among musicians as common time. For a musician, to be on beat is the goal and to be off beat is usually, but not always, bad because the audience can't follow the rhythm.

Screenwriters often lay out their script using a tool called a beat sheet. It is useful to employ a beat sheet structure for planning out your grant proposal and I like to use it for identifying the emotional beats to hit in each grant section. A grant writer can also use the concept of beats to drive the rhythm of their narrative. In this sample beat sheet, I list the key components of a grant as beats.

A grant reader participates in training provided by the funding agency on the RFA before they are allowed to begin reading grants. In the training, the readers learn the beats (grant sections) of the grant they are about to score. It is important to understand that the readers read your grant according to these beats. While the actual beats you find in any RFA may vary a little from the design presented here, the grant beats included are typical. Should you fail to follow the RFA outline and get offbeat, you will surely sacrifice points and fail to receive funding.

A brief summary of each grant beat is included below. In order to create a more meaningful narrative, it is helpful to list emotive details you want to include. An emotive detail might be something meaningful about the needs that makes them quintessential, it may be an important characteristic of your hero, it may be a supportive partnership, or it could be methods to include a diverse stakeholder group.

Grant Beat Sheet	Troll Grant Emotive Details
Abstract – The key emotion this section should elicit is excitement about reading the rest of the proposal. Hook them with the state of misfortune, summarize the goals and objectives, explain how that the new higher state will be evaluated. The entire grant narrative is summarized within this section so it needs to be tightly written and hard-hitting.	
Opening – This is a summary of the abstract that gives context to the first section. One paragraph giving the name of the hero, the point of the project, how many victims will be saved from the state of misfortune.	
The Needs – These are the details about the needs/problem that should elicit empathy, sympathy, anger, frustration, even sadness. This is where your reader should be sighing heavily and perhaps even reaching for the Kleenex. The entire narrative grows from this point forward so only include the problems that the quest will resolve. Don't raise false emotions and then let them down by not addressing them.	
Who We Are – The needs should transition to the design section by giving a brief description of the hero who will resolve the problem. The emotional impact should be admiration and confidence.	
Goals and Objectives – The key emotions to hit in this section are approval, satisfaction, and complicity. The reader feels terrible that the victims are facing this state of misfortune and they already have ideas about how they would resolve the needs. The goals and objectives should make them say, "That's what I would do, or that is a great idea I didn't think of, let's get busy here and fund this plan."	

The Program Design – The emotions to hit here are confidence, inspiration, innovation, admiration, and wonder. The plan is laid out in this section and the emotions are tapped by the logic of the solutions, the validity of the actions to be taken, the quality of the hero that will implement the solutions, and the brilliance of the innovations. The reader wants to go with you if your needs raise the requisite emotions in them.	
Management Plan – The management plan builds on the confidence established in the design section. You are satisfying the skeptics among your readers who are thinking, "OK, I like everything I'm hearing, but do they REALLY know what they're doing?" If you slip up at this point in the narrative, the reader could fall into despair about the plan and underlying fears about giving the talisman to you will overtake their desire to join the quest. You can't afford to let them down here, even though by this time you are weary of searching your brain for details.	
Evaluation – This section is where you bring your reader into that higher state, ecstasy. Your description of the ways you are going to measure the success of the program design will delight and amaze them. Here, you will put the final touches on their confidence about your ability to measure, adjust and report, and your willingness toward accountability.	
Budget and Sustaining Effort – The budget should inspire admiration and confidence. It should be clean and flawless encouraging your readers to recommend funding. It should never provoke shock by being over the stated budget limit, and it should not include surprise line items that cause the reader to say, "What are they buying that for?" or "Why wasn't that described in the narrative?" It should also never include calculation errors!	

Made in the USA
Las Vegas, NV
16 November 2022

59618436R00104